A Practical Approach to Business Impact Analysis

A Practical Approach to Business Impact Analysis

Understanding the Organization through Business Continuity Management

Ian Charters

First published in the UK in 2011 by BSI, 389 Chiswick High Road, London W4 4AL

Typeset in Great Britain by Letterpart Limited - letterpart.com
Printed in Great Britain by Berforts Group, www.berforts.co.uk

British Library Cataloguing in Publication Data
A catalogue record for this book is available from the British Library

ISBN 978-0-580-73101-3

Contents

Acknowledgements

I am grateful to fellow BCM professionals, particularly on BSI's BCM/1 Committee, who have listened carefully to my views on Business Impact Analysis and challenged them constructively.

I am particularly indebted to Mel Gosling MBCI for his insightful comments on the draft drawn from his wide experience; some of his practical tips appear in the text. Lyndon Bird FBCI made some very useful suggestions, and thanks too to Jim Grafton AMBCI for his detailed review of the text from the perspective of a user.

I am also grateful to Gillian Charters and Eleanor Sharpston for a detailed sense check of the text.

Foreword

Business Impact Analysis (BIA) is the technique that is so closely associated with Business Continuity Management (BCM) that many think of them as virtually the same thing. In this excellent review of the mysteries of BIA, Ian Charters treats everyone from the BCM newcomer to the seasoned professional to a "tour de force" of this often misunderstood topic. To many, it is axiomatic that you cannot develop an effective BCM programme unless it is based upon a precise and comprehensive BIA. However to others, the BIA is seen as little more than a financial model to cost-justify an expensive technical recovery solution. Even worse, some see it as simply an exercise to over analyse a business to a point where management lose interest and no effective BCM is implemented.

This book dispels all such myths in a readable and surprisingly jargon-free manner. Ian Charters quotes from nearly 20 years of practical experience in undertaking BIAs for international clients in all shapes and sizes. He shows that the mathematical precision demanded by some companies in measuring impacts is both impossible and unnecessary, he shows that there are many ways in which the BIA can help determine appropriate recovery strategies and he constantly warns about the danger of over analysing, taking too long and failing to take management with you.

There is no 'one size fits all' way of carrying out a successful BIA and as such no single methodology that will work in all cases. However there are pitfalls that can be avoided with the help of an expert who has done it all many times before. The real life examples scattered throughout this book are eye-openers with lessons to be learned from each of them. The author has also taken on a number of contentious subjects with candour and well argued conclusions. In particular the role of Risk Management in BCM, the value of national and international standards and the role external consultants will probably lead to some intense debate around the BCM conference circuit.

This book is thought provoking as well as highly informative and might be destined to become the definitive guide on how to conduct an effective BIA. I enjoyed it enormously and feel sure fellow BCM professionals will share my enthusiasm.

Lyndon Bird FBCI
International Technical Director
The Business Continuity Institute

A Practical Approach to Business Impact Analysis

Preface

> 'The Business Impact Analysis is the backbone of the entire business continuity exercise ... or at least it should be'
>
> *Bill Meredith, FBCI – one of the founders of the Business Continuity Institute*

I was fortunate to undertake my first Business Impact Analysis (BIA) before I knew anything about business continuity. Back in 1993 I was tasked with answering an apparently simple question by a petrochemical company: 'Do we need a disaster recovery (DR) contract for our mainframe computer, because we are tired of being chased by salesmen?'. Unfettered by existing methods to answer the question and using my experience as a business analyst, I suggested we ask each of the business areas how quickly the lack of computer systems would cause them significant difficulties, and why. The answers were a surprise. The most urgent process that depended on computer systems was that of a ship, loaded and ready to sail, listing a full ship's cargo for the captain (a bill of lading), which was required within 20 minutes (before the tide started to go out and the ship grounded); the next most urgent activity could wait several weeks. Further research showed that the bill of lading application, if not completed correctly, could shut down oil production across several oil fields since no one had ever considered the implications of its failure. Severe impacts within days could also result from telecommunications failure – which had been outside the original project scope – and there were no working alternative routes.

Convinced I had worked out an original way of looking at a business, I was rather disappointed to find that others had addressed these issues too and were calling it Business Continuity (BC) – what has now become Business Continuity Management (BCM). The simplicity of the method I had devised for that original project has remained, though the questions are now asked about the whole organization rather than just computer systems. This experience also reminds us of the need to be inquisitive when trying to understand the workings of an organization and to ask even apparently stupid questions if things don't make sense. Because everyone else in the business tends to work in departmental silos, at the end of the first BIA you will almost certainly know the organization's whole operation better than anyone within it – a very powerful position!

Since then I have undertaken the first BIAs for many organizations in a wide variety of sectors using the same approach, but refining the method each time to fit the organization's unique character. More recently, I have had the opportunity to embed a BIA programme within organizations following the ideas outlined in this volume. I have also had the benefit of discussing these ideas with fellow BCM professionals whilst working on BS 25999 and ISO 22301 and ISO/CD 22313 BCM Standards, which have convinced me of the need to set out a practical approach to the issues to support their requirements.

For several years I have run a training course on Business Impact Analysis as part of a suite of training courses on many aspects of BCM. The challenge of explaining the principles of BIA in one day to delegates from a wide variety of organizations is behind the approach in this text. I am grateful to the hundreds of delegates that have taken this course for allowing me to take up that challenge. There is nothing that tests the logic of a process better than trying to explain it to an intelligent and motivated group who know that they will be expected to apply the training on their return to the office.

My hope is that this text – based on real experience, which includes some setbacks – will give the reader confidence and sufficient guidance to embark on the often fascinating quest to find out how their organization really works.

Ian Charters
Fellow of the Business Continuity Institute
Director, Continuity Systems Ltd

About the author

Ian Charters is a specialist in all aspects of Business Continuity Management with a client profile covering many sectors and organisation sizes. He was accepted as a Member of the Business Continuity Institute in 1997, elected a Fellow in 2004 and served as a Board member 2001–7. He is a member of BSI's BCM/1 Committee and a UK expert appointed to ISO TC223.

He has experience in a wide range of sectors having undertaken BCM projects in the finance, insurance, logistics, manufacturing and public sectors. He specialises in undertaking BIAs and ensures that the organisation can develop an appropriate BCM programme from the results.

Ian is a skilled training presenter and has delivered courses on BIA and other BCM topics in the UK, Cyprus and the Middle and Far East. This book is derived from the successful BIA course run regularly in the UK.

Introduction

The aim of this book

For a topic as important to a discipline as BIA is to BCM, there is remarkably little written on the subject or available on the internet. There are templates available, both for free and for payment, but few explorations of the wider issues that are needed to make effective use of those templates even within the sector for which they were designed. This is because it is difficult, in a few pages, to describe the process of BIA and show its applicability in all sectors. In addition, the BIA method used by external consultants to initiate a BCM programme may appear to bear little relation to the BIA process embedded in the processes of more BCM-mature organizations.

This book is not going to present the reader with a 'one size fits all' template for undertaking a BIA in every sector. Blindly following a template is unlikely to result in a meaningful result. Instead readers are invited to think through the guidance offered, consider the purpose of the data they will collect and devise their own BIA method which fits the current and future needs of their business.

About this book

The term 'Business Impact Analysis' has been applied to a wide variety of different methods over the years but a consensus has emerged in the last few years following the publication of BS 25999-1, *Business continuity management — Code of practice*, BS 25999-2, *Business continuity management — Specification* and, more recently, ASIS/BSI (BCM.01:2010). An international standard is yet to be published but ISO/DIS 22301 suggests that the approach in the earlier standards will be adopted. The methods that support the implementation of these standards are described in the Business Continuity Institute's *Good Practice Guidelines 2010 (GPG 2010)*, which is regularly updated to reflect current practice.

The scope of this book covers the topic 'Business Impact Analysis' that is described (with minor variations) in these standards and guidance. In BS 25999 and the *GPG 2010* the 'Continuity Requirements Analysis' is described as a separate step but, because this collection of resource requirements is usually undertaken at the same time as a BIA, this has been included in the scope of this text.

It has been assumed that there is top management support for undertaking a BIA; if not, then efforts need to be made to gain this support first, a topic not covered here.

The first chapter presents a definition of BIA, explains its importance in the BCM Programme and sets the context in which it is performed.

The second chapter examines the concepts and terminology of the BIA. The reader may prefer to skip this chapter, referring back to it from later chapters when further explanation is required.

The third chapter describes two approaches to undertaking a BIA. A project approach is usually adopted for an initial BIA. Once a BCM programme is established, the BIA can become a process, split into a number of linked activities that are embedded in the organization's management procedures.

The next three chapters discuss how to conduct the BIA as part of a programme using the 'Strategic, Tactical and Operational' model. Those undertaking a first BIA are likely to include elements of all these in coming to an initial understanding of the organization.

The final chapter shows how the results from the BIA project or programme provide the information on which the appropriate BCM strategies can be selected and effective recovery plans developed.

Having said that, no universal template can be provided; Appendix 1 contains a cross reference to the various topics in the text from which readers can, if they wish, create a template for use within their organization.

Throughout this book two icons are used to help you find what you need:

Real-life examples describing tried and tested approaches

Key points

1   What is Business Impact Analysis?

A definition

The BCI's Glossary, BS 25999 and ISO/DIS 22301 all define a BIA as 'the process of analysing business functions and the effect that a business disruption might have upon them'; the ASIS/BSI BCM.01 2010 definition is very similar.

To understand the effect of a disruption a BIA needs to ask:

- What are the key business/service objectives of the organization?
- What products and services are required to meet these objectives of the organization? (Deliverables)
- How are the objectives going to be achieved? (Activities)
- Who and what needs to be involved (both internally and externally) to achieve the objectives? (Resources)
- (And most crucially) When do these objectives need to be achieved? (Time)

These questions are standard business analysis queries but only in the BIA does the last question – relating to time – play such a key role.

A BIA looks at each product, service, process and activity within the organization, understands its significance to the organization and determines the impacts over time that would result if it were to be disrupted.

It also documents the interdependencies of the activities within a business and with suppliers of goods and services. It is necessary to understand this complexity to make estimates of the impacts over time of a disruption to back office and corporate activities.

Once the impacts have been determined, the maximum tolerable period of disruption (MTPD) can then be estimated by asking how long it will be before the continuing failure to carry out the activity will create intolerable impacts.

Why is a BIA so important?

It is necessary to undertake a BIA to understand how quickly the organization needs to respond when a disruption to normal business occurs. It becomes a statement of requirements for the recovery strategy following a disruption. By knowing how quickly the delivery of the various products and services needs to be restored, we can work out how quickly the various activities within and outside the business need to be recovered to enable that to happen.

If these recovery requirements are guessed at, without a BIA process, we could set recovery objectives but when an incident occurs these might be either an:

- underestimate – leading to the organization suffering severe or terminal damage as it could not meet the time or scale of recovery demanded by its customers even though there was a plan; or an
- overestimate – and the organization would continually be spending sums of money on recovery capabilities that were not required, making it uncompetitive or inefficient.

> **Sometimes there is a limit to how long customers will wait**: Following a fire, a manufacturing company rebuilt its plant with the insurance payout, but within six months it had closed because its customers had taken their custom elsewhere and, on resumption of production, too few were won back from their competitors to make the new plant profitable.
> **Sometimes the need for a speedy recovery is overestimated**: A government department was paying a supplier to provide a 4-hour on-site response to multiple locations. To achieve this, the supplier had several mobile facilities in various places enabling it to fulfil this contractual requirement. However, for various reasons, an incident went unresolved for 36 hours but there were no serious repercussions of this delay. The contract was renegotiated to 36 hours, which required just one mobile unit, thus saving a substantial sum.

So the BIA will enable the organization to select an appropriate approach to, and a detailed strategy for, business resumption after a disruption. In times of financial pressure and in the public sector it is particularly important to demonstrate this close match between requirements and spending.

Once the strategy is selected, the BIA can even assist us in working out how long an 'escalating' incident can be left until the plan is invoked. This decision of when to act (for example, to move to an alternative location) is particularly difficult in situations where the problem is temporary, such as a power failure or denial of access.

The BIA also provides an opportunity to make managers more aware of the need for BCM and how it affects their role.

The BIA is conventionally used to determine the current recovery requirements of an organization. It can also be used to consider the impact of disruption under other assumptions. So an organization considering a major change, such as relocation or reorganization, could use the BIA to identify which configurations, from a number of possibilities, provide the required resilience.

What are the prerequisites?

It should be obvious that it is necessary to obtain the full support of the organization's senior management before starting a BIA. Attempts to speak to managers may be rebuffed unless this support is forthcoming. It also needs to be 'sold' to managers as being of interest to them as individuals and an explanatory note in advance of a meeting (described later – see Chapter 5) should address both requirements.

It may be premature to launch into a BIA before there is a semblance of a BCM programme in place. A BIA conducted by an external consultancy may fail to be followed up if there is no identified individual within the organization to learn from the BIA and implement the solutions required by its findings.

Training of people to plan and undertake a BIA – whether classroom-based or self-study – on BCM and particularly on the BIA method, is essential to ensure that the process is effective. Even if an external specialist is being employed, it will be useful for in-house personnel to receive training so they can assist the specialist to understand their organization and take the learning forward when the external specialist leaves.

Undertaking a BCM exercise with the senior management in advance of the formal BIA may be useful. Exploring their reaction to a disruption will achieve:

*   an appreciation of the need for a BCM programme by the senior management – so buy-in for the BIA will be enhanced;
*   an initial understanding of the business – especially the products, services and the major stakeholders as perceived by management;
*   a preliminary acceptance of the context and scope of the BIA, if this has not yet been decided.

In an ideal BCM programme, a BIA should be undertaken using the scope (or a subset of the scope) as set out in the BCM Policy. However, if a policy is not yet agreed, a BIA may be a valuable tool to gain a sufficient understanding of the organization to enable the scope of a BCM Policy to be drafted.

BIA scope

The scope of a BIA should be defined in terms of products or services since, at the strategic level, it is primarily about customer response. The term 'product and service' is shorthand for a wide variety of options which can include:

- a group of products or services which have similar characteristics;
- a single product (or group) delivered to a single customer;
- products supplied to a specific geographical area (where one possible strategy is to provide the product from another area).

When using a wide geographical scope it can prove difficult to explain how all sites are unable to operate where the product or service is produced from several sites. However, industrial action or picketing at all sites is one of several scenarios that could cause this.

Selecting just one customer may make it difficult to identify how much resource is required to operate activities that provide support to other customers or products.

Some methods suggest limiting the scope of the BIA by a 'planning horizon', such as a length of disruption beyond which impacts are not considered. It is difficult, however, to see how either the impacts or the appropriate horizon can be determined in advance of the BIA process.

Where an organization has several production locations and a dispersed customer base it may be difficult to identify an appropriate geographical scope of the BIA. One of the following may be appropriate:

- whole organization, where the various locations are strongly interdependent – there may be a lower-level 'Sub-strategic' BIA for each significant location set within the overall Strategic BIA;
- one (or a group of locations), where the locations are fairly autonomous and each serves a discrete geographical area;
- identifying what is delivered to different regions, as separate products or services which can be included or excluded from the scope.

The best choice for scope is often guided by the likely structure of the BCM strategy and incident response, whether this is to be centralised or locally managed.

2 Understanding the BIA

This chapter outlines the concepts, terminology and methods of the BIA.

Time and impact

Why is time everything in managing incidents?

When an unexpected incident occurs that affects an organization there may be disruption to its operations. As a result, the supply of products or services to customers may be interrupted. This may be noticed quickly if the disruption affects the 'front office' activities, or more slowly if it is the support or back office processes, such as accounts, that are affected.

The cause of the incident and its immediate impacts will determine the initial response. If it is an emergency, such as a fire or explosion, the emergency services may initially take control of the situation. The incident may create some initial sympathy and understanding from customers if the cause of the problem lies outside the organization's control. However, this sympathy disappears quite quickly if the organization fails to restore the service to customers, who will blame the organization, not for the incident but for the inadequacy of response and the tardiness of service restoration.

So, whereas the plans for the initial response to an incident need to take into account its cause, the plans and timetable for recovering the organization's operations are determined by the demands of customers and the impacts on other stakeholders irrespective of the cause of the disruption. Thus we need to understand the impacts and timescales of a disruption, in advance, to determine the likely priorities after the incident – and how long the disruption can last before the organization's survival is threatened.

There are three interacting elements that determine this survival point – collectively known as the maximum tolerable period of disruption (MTPD):

- the stakeholders who suffer the impacts;
- the nature and size of the impacts on those stakeholders;
- the rate at which those impacts grow over time.

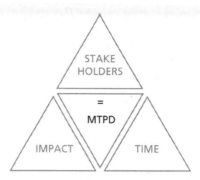

Figure 1   The elements that determine the maximum tolerable period of disruption

Stakeholder identification

It is useful to conduct a stakeholder analysis as part of the BIA process because the impacts of a disruptive incident will affect a number of stakeholders and the effectiveness of the organization's recovery will be judged by all of these.

For the purpose of the BIA, stakeholders can be divided into four broad groups:

1. Within the organization:
   - the staff and executive directors
2. In the market sector:
   - customers and partners
   - competitors
3. Those with a financial interest:
   - suppliers
   - shareholders
   - the organization's bank or other financiers
   - the organization's insurance companies
4. Those with other interests in the organization's affairs:
   - staff families
   - neighbours
   - politicians
   - the media
   - pressure groups

Although the main focus of the BIA will be the impact on customers, the impact on each of the other stakeholders should be considered.

- What is their interest?
- How will a disruption affect them, and over what timescale?
- How could it be mitigated before and after the incident?

This will give a fuller appreciation of the impacts and will provide useful information to assist in the development of a Communications Plan as part of the BCM response.

The reaction of stakeholders must be anticipated in determining the impact of the disruption – and it may not be the obvious one, as in the following examples.

- One owner/director of a small business dismissed my suggestion that a BC plan was required – he said he would retire on the insurance payout.
- In some sectors competing businesses co-operate during a disruption (for instance, financial services during the London bombings in the 1990s) because they see the stability of the sector as more important than taking advantage of the situation to increase market share.
- Where the public's reaction to a disruption causes a response from politicians, they may then threaten changes to legislation which may affect both the public and commercial sectors.
- The owners of a factory assumed they would be able to quickly rebuild on the site if there was a fire, but the neighbours could prevent this once they became aware that lethal chemicals were being stored and used there.

Defining the 'customer'

The 'customer' is a special member of the stakeholder group since it is to the customer that an organization supplies its products and services and whose patience will be tried if a disruption interrupts that delivery.

Commercial organizations

The identification of 'customers' is relatively straightforward in commercial organizations – they receive the goods or services and pay the invoices.

Some commercial organizations will need to consider, in addition, potential customers either because of a long pre-sales process or because there is a high turnover of customers (such as one-off purchases). These potential customers may be less tolerant of a disruption than existing customers with whom there is already a working relationship.

It may be also useful to consider bodies such as regulators as a 'customer' in that they may expect to receive timely information and there is usually a group of people undertaking an activity within the organization that collates and delivers this information.

Not for profit organizations

Business Continuity is as relevant to not-for-profit organizations as it is for commercial businesses and this is reflected in various attempts to use different names for BCM, such as Service Continuity. Throughout this text there are references to 'customer'; this may need to be clarified for those in the not-for-profit sector.

In government agencies – such as local authorities and benefit agencies – the term 'customer' may refer to the electorate or to the section of it to whom the services (housing support, waste collection, etc.) are provided. Within government itself the organization's customer may instead be the politicians or other representatives to whom services (legislation preparation, expenses etc.) are provided.

For charities, the customer is more difficult to describe. The donors to whom the charity would be answerable for the effective use of their donation could be considered as customers, but it may also be helpful to consider potential donors as well as any regulatory or oversight body to whom information is provided. The beneficiaries of the charity could also be seen as customers though. For medical charities undertaking research, this may be many years in the future.

The nature of impacts

When an organization's operation is disrupted there can be a number of interrelated impacts across a wide variety of stakeholders.

Within the market:

- The customer will not receive the service expected and may react by withholding payment or demanding compensation or contract penalties.
- Some customers may take advantage of the situation and delay payments so increasing bad debts.
- The organization's reputation for competence may be under threat.
- Customers may cancel future orders and potential customers may be lost.
- The loss of the service could have health or safety implications for the public.
- The organization cannot take advantage of opportunities and may lose its competitive edge.
- Competitors may see an opportunity for capturing customers or even taking over the enterprise.
- Regulators may be concerned about the trading position or competence of the organization to operate within compliance requirements and may impose financial penalties if these are breached.

Those providing finance and other resources:

- The organization's bank may be concerned about the security of its loan and demand its immediate repayment.
- The cost of restoration and the additional costs of working may require significant borrowing and may incur high interest payments.
- Shareholders may be concerned about a drop in share price and may sell their shares.
- The insurers may be concerned about their liability after an incident and force the organization down a particular recovery route.
- Suppliers will be concerned that payment will not be made for goods or services supplied and will require accounts to be settled or cash paid in advance for a continuing supply.

Within the organization:

- Staff will be concerned about their salary being paid on time and even the security of their jobs. As a result their motivation may be affected and key personnel may leave the organization.
- The loss of revenue from lost production or bad debts may threaten the organization's viability.
- The additional costs of working – overdraft charges, extra transport, overtime and costs of restoration – may threaten viability.
- The safety of the working environment may be reduced.
- Management credibility may be damaged.
- Key projects may be delayed or cancelled.
- Long-term strategic plans may be derailed.

Other interests:

- Politicians or pressure groups may see an opportunity to further their agendas.
- The incident may have created actual or threatened environmental damage.
- Litigation resulting from the incident can have a prolonged impact on reputation.
- The incident is likely to generate media interest both at the time of the incident and for some while afterwards. It is likely to be revisited when a similar incident occurs.

These impacts can be evaluated in their own right – for example, how quickly will the organization's cash run out? Or they can be analysed as indirect reasons why the delivery of products to customers will cease – for example, suppliers cancelling deliveries of components or staff taking industrial action because they have not been paid.

The nature of the impacts will vary considerably between sectors. The failure of air traffic control or life support systems in a hospital could have potentially fatal consequences. In a financial institution a delay may cost huge sums of money. The failure to deliver on a contract may have huge reputational impact usually dwarfing any financial penalties.

The last example is not intended to imply that delivery on contracts cannot be delayed or agreed service levels breached. Some degradation in service to customers may be tolerable for a limited period with the approval of top management.

Measuring impacts

As already stated, the BIA is attempting to measure the impact of a disruption over time. So finding a scale of measurement for those impacts may appear to be a requirement.

In a risk analysis, impacts resulting from a business disruption are usually classified on a scale such as 1–5 or 'low', 'medium' and 'high'. This appears to provide a way of recording the 'impacts' on a common scale across the organization, and one that could be used by the BIA, thus providing a link between these two disciplines. However, attempting to estimate impact without a time parameter omits the crucial relationship between these two. In addition, the use of a numeric scale, such as 1–5, implies an arithmetic relationship between the scales of the impacts; yet, for example, a level 2 incident is often defined as much less than half the impact of a level 4. This will overstate the importance of the low-impact incidents. The definitions of the relative costs of each level of damage often match a geometric or logarithmic progression more closely.

The nature of many of the impacts described above make it impossible to use a common financial scale. Often where there is a known financial cost, such as a penalty or fine, then the reputational damage associated with having incurred that penalty is much more damaging, and its impacts can continue for some time after the event.

Some BIA methods base their calculation of impact on estimates of the monetary cost of loss of an individual department or business process. This ignores the complex interrelationships between the various parts of an organization as well as the complexity of the impacts. It is just not possible to quantify in isolation the cost of disruption in, for example, the human resources department.

This complexity and the intangible nature of many of the impacts means that any attempt to identify the costs of an interruption in advance is likely to be time consuming; some impact lists run to around 100 items to evaluate. However rigorously such quantification is attempted, it is likely to significantly understate, perhaps by as much as a factor of ten, the actual costs experienced after an incident because of the many intangibles and imponderables.

> In the early hours of 5th July 2010 DBS Bank of Singapore suffered a breakdown of their IT infrastructure which disrupted banking services at DBS branches and its ATM machines causing what the Monetary Authority of Singapore (MAS) termed 'significant inconvenience to the bank's customers'. In a statement, MAS 'censured DBS for the shortcomings and inadequate management oversight by the bank of its outsourced IT systems, networks, operations and infrastructure' ... and asked the bank to set aside an additional S\$230 million in regulatory capital.

(from The Straits Times, August 4th 2010)

The conclusion has to be drawn that attempting to calculate accurately the financial costs of an incident in advance is impossible and the BIA cannot therefore be a purely numerical exercise. For the purposes of selecting strategies it is only necessary to know when these impacts become intolerable for the organization – that is, when they threaten its short- or long-term viability.

So a pair of terms can be used to indicate this threshold: the impact is either 'tolerable' or it is 'intolerable'. These terms are sufficiently general to accommodate in their meaning the cumulative impact of financial costs, reputational damage and even mortality. But this generality does mean that top managers need to make the strategic decisions on tolerability since only they have the knowledge, overall perspective and responsibility to decide how much impact the organization can tolerate. The prospect of potentially having to defend that decision to the media should focus top management's mind when presented with the costs of a recovery strategy.

This tolerance to impact may change over time as the organization's financial and reputational stability changes. It may also change dramatically after a disruption which may plunder both its cash and goodwill reserves, making it more vulnerable should a second incident occur.

The relationship between impact and time

Adverts for resilient IT 'solutions' often pose the question: 'Do you realise that each hour of disruption costs you \$nnn' which suggests that there is a linear relationship between impact and time. However, this does not accurately represent the complex relationship between these two parameters.

Whatever the cause, the cumulative impact of an incident, if not managed, always increases over time but not in a simple relationship.

Impacts may rise continuously, periodically or uncertainly – a concept that needs to be understood when deciding when these impacts could become 'intolerable'.

Continuous impacts

For those organizations that deliver 'always available' services – such as internet service providers, utilities and e-commerce – the impact of a disruption will be felt immediately. Revenue losses are likely to be immediate and increase relatively regularly. Most organizations intend to be always available, but only during the working day, although they may also choose to consider these impacts as of a continuous nature (treating a failure out of hours as good fortune).

Periodic impacts

Some organizations have periodic deadlines which, if not met, can cause impacts to increase suddenly. For example:

- periodic peaks and troughs in service delivery, such as in taxation call centres at the financial year end or at universities enrolling students at the start of the academic year;
- external reporting deadlines, such as daily stock market valuations or delivery of annual reports;
- contractual times at which penalty clauses in contracts are triggered and fines become payable;
- the publication of a damaging press story can have a sudden impact on the reputation of an organization.

Uncertain impacts

The most problematic decisions about impacts and time are those where the outcome of a disruption may lead to an intolerable situation but it is not certain if or when this situation will arise, as in the following examples.

- The failure of an ambulance control centre will at some point lead to an avoidable death but this could be within minutes, hours or days depending on when the emergency occurs to which the service cannot respond.
- A stock trading system failure could have limited impact on a day of minimal trading, but could have a huge impact if the markets are volatile.
- Within an organization, if ICT support and facilities management are absent, there may be no impact unless, or until, something goes wrong which requires their intervention.

Impacts are cumulative

Because impacts are cumulative, as shown in Figure 2, the decision on what constitutes a maximum tolerable impact should take into account the aggregate of all types of impact that might result from the disruption.

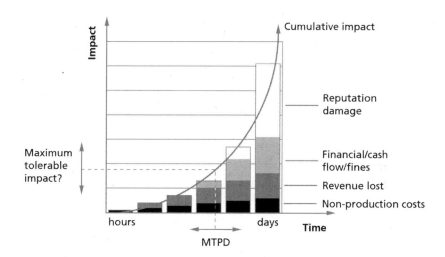

Figure 2   How the components of impact grow over time

Significant time periods in recovery options

With so many factors to consider, it is clear that quantification of impact and time can only be approximate. However, the time parameters of the available recovery strategies are similarly approximate, as is demonstrated by the examples below.

The options for recovery of office-based activities are usually limited to:

- doing nothing in advance – but recovery may take months to achieve because of the complexities of leasing buildings and arranging utility connections;
- relocation to an unprepared or temporary building – which can be made ready for occupation in a few weeks (often called a 'cold site');
- relocation to a prepared site – which can be operational in days as all facilities, equipment and furniture are in place (often called a 'warm site');
- running an activity from two or more diverse locations – which can enable recovery immediately or within hours depending on which data replication solutions are in place.

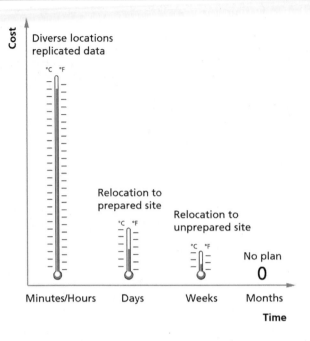

Figure 3   Recovery options against cost and time

For coping with loss of staff, depending on the skill level required, the options could be:

- recruitment – but this could take months;
- using agency staff – but training might take days;
- redeploying staff – this might take hours or days depending on their location and training;
- moving work to other staff already undertaking this activity, perhaps elsewhere – this might be accomplished immediately, or within minutes or hours, depending on the technology in place.

For coping with IT loss the options are, in general terms:

- buy nothing in advance – with equipment taking from days to months to replace depending on its complexity and availability; networks may take months to install depending on the capacity and service agreements of the provider;
- third party sites are able to deliver contracted equipment to sites within hours;
- restoring data from back-up media may take hours to days even with an alternative data centre immediately available and fully equipped;
- high availability, replicated systems – with recovery times in seconds or minutes.

From these examples above a key point emerges:

> Because the purpose of the BIA is, principally, to identify appropriate recovery strategies then it need only determine whether the disruption must be over within seconds, hours, days, weeks or months. This accuracy is sufficient to be able to choose the appropriate recovery strategy. Given the complexity of the factors further accuracy should be viewed with scepticism.

Double whammies

The widespread incident scenario (such as a pandemic) has a further complication. With customers also affected, the demands on the organization may be expected to reduce more quickly than the organization's capabilities to meet them – in which case the situation is manageable. However, in certain sectors the nature of the incident and customer's reaction to it may lead to levels of demand above normal. In a pandemic, for example, health care, life insurance (claims) and mail order companies may all experience increased demand in a situation where they may also be struggling as a result of staff absence and supply issues.

Emergency response organizations are particularly vulnerable to these double hits. They are expected to respond to widespread incidents at a level beyond their normal capacity but their communications infrastructure, staff, buildings and other resources may be unavailable because of the incident – such as in the case of a flood or severe weather.

> In a flooded city, the police were desperate for wellington boots, but the manager of the police stores (in which there were plenty of 'wellies') had sent his staff away early and shut the stores because he expected a flood would make it difficult for staff to get home!

BIA and culture

As BIA findings are strongly influenced by customer and other stakeholder behaviour, it is obvious that timescales derived for an organization in one country may not be applicable for branches of the organization in other countries. Attitudes to contracts, agreements and the enforcement of penalties differ between countries and cultures. This can make the determination of tolerable timescales for international business relationships particularly challenging.

Terminology

Activity and process

One of the most difficult issues in conducting a BIA is to decide on the level of detail to use to analyse the business. A simple organization with a few staff may be easily described by a few processes which deliver a service and others which provide administrative support. A multinational organization will deliver many products and services through thousands of processes across the world. This makes it difficult to describe a common method of analysis for such diverse organizations.

The approach in this text is to use the term 'activity' to refer to a business operation with identified inputs, outputs and resource requirements within a department, which directly or indirectly support the production of the organization's goods or services. A department's recovery plan will be documented to recover these activities.

In a large organization it may be useful to identify higher level processes, made up of a number of activities, some of which may involve several departments. In this text this group of activities is described as a 'process'. A process is likely to be defined as the level of detail at which those responsible for developing and invoking the recovery plan of the organization will work.

In a small organization these two levels of detail may not be required, in which case process and activity can be merged. For this reason the terms 'process' and 'activity' have been used flexibly within the text.

In a small organization the paying of suppliers may be a process undertaken by one or two individuals and therefore requires no further analysis.
In a large organization this process may be made up of a number of linked activities undertaken by several individuals in different departments, such as:

- recording the supplier invoice (accounts);
- checking the invoice against items received (user departments);
- checking against contract (procurement);
- scheduling for payment (accounts);
- printing cheque and mailing it (mail room).

The terms 'function' and 'operation' have been avoided because they often have special meanings within organizations which, if used, could lead to confusion with embedded nomenclature.

Figure 4a   An organization analysed by processes

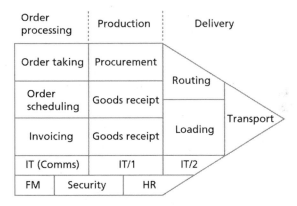

Figure 4b   An organization analysed by activities within processes

Figure 4a shows a (simplified) organization described by three processes delivering one product. This may be an appropriate abstraction at which to understand how products and services are delivered. At the next stage, shown in Figure 4b, the activities that make up the processes are identified. A process may cut across several departments, but to make it easier to assign resources to an activity, it should be wholly contained within a department. In the first BIA it may not be immediately apparent which processes and activities should be identified and, in practice, this may not become apparent until departmental recovery plans are being drawn up. Changes in the organization are likely to require adjustments to this classification.

An organization's legal team of nine staff put their legal training to work when defining the activities within their department. They identified 12 separate activities (with considerable detail), of which only two had an MTPD of less than two weeks. Some consolidation was agreed upon of the other ten activities into three; further consolidation of their detailed effort might have lost their good will.

When undertaking a BIA, an organization can choose to define a process and activity in whatever way is appropriate to understand its operation and use whatever terms will be meaningful.

If a BIA appears to be too big an undertaking or is taking too long, it is probably because it is going into too much detail by defining too many separate processes. It is easier to break down a process into activities at a later stage than trying to generalize lots of activity detail into one process afterwards.

In practice, a single site organization may be described adequately by around 20 processes, and a department might be analysed on anything from one to ten activities, depending on its size and complexity. The more separate the processes and activities, the more complex the BIA and, eventually, the recovery plan will be; this should act as a constraint on the depth of analysis. The detail of the analysis should also decrease as the MTPD increases – so it may be appropriate to create a 'miscellaneous' activity in each department that can include all the low urgency tasks that need not be separately identified or recovered individually.

Maximum tolerable period of disruption (MTPD)

The assumption on which the BIA method is based is that, if the disruption continues, at some point in time the damage to an organization will be so significant that recovery becomes impossible. It may not reopen after the disruption, but even if operations are restored, its reputation and finances may have been damaged so much that it loses customers, becomes unviable and then closes or is taken over.

Most organizations provide more than one product or service, so the BIA assumes that each product and service has its own threshold beyond which recovery will not be possible. The top management need to identify, roughly, these tipping points by deciding the extent of the maximum tolerable impact of disruption the organization can absorb and, from this estimate, the time period after a disruption at which this impact will occur.

MTPD was a term first introduced in BS 25999-1. It came about as an attempt to formulate guidance for setting planned recovery times, and thus BCM recovery strategies in the next stage of the programme. It was argued that you cannot set realistic recovery times unless you are aware of the point in time beyond which you cannot recover. Although the term does not appear in ISO/DIS 22301 the concept is still present in the requirement to take into consideration the time within which the impacts of not resuming them would become unacceptable.

Inevitably the MTPD is an approximation. As explained above, it is rarely possible to be much more specific than to decide on its unit of measure – for example, minutes, hours, days or months. Indeed, excessive accuracy should be viewed with suspicion. However, its approximation should not cast doubt on its existence as a phenomenon. Without it, the temptation will be to base a decision on recovery timescales on what appears to be achievable at the time, but this could turn out to be too slow. There will be a point at which even the most loyal customers leave if the organization fails to deliver.

The MTPD can be defined as the period between the incident and the approximate point in time at which recovery is pointless or impossible because the cumulative impacts have damaged the organization so much that it will not recover (though the actual costs of these impacts may take some time to manifest themselves). Damage to reputation, for example, can cause a long-term impact on sales and staff morale long after the disruption is over – which is often why organizations actually fail some time after the incident that has caused their demise.

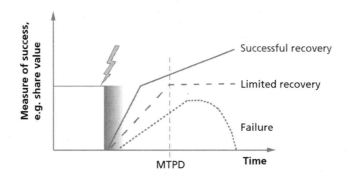

Figure 5   The relationship between time and organizational survival after a disruption

Figure 5 shows three theoretical outcomes of an incident (a bolt of lightning in this case) disrupting an organization's operation. The dotted line shows an organization attempting to recover but by the MTPD it is not back to its previous state so it loses its momentum and fails. The dashed line describes an organization that just recovers in time; in theory it will just survive. The solid line shows an organization that recovers comfortably before the MTPD and may well do better after the incident as its reputation is enhanced and its staff morale is boosted by the success of the recovery.

Phased recovery

In BS 25999-1:2006 (sub-clause 6.2.2) the clarity of a single threshold or tipping point has been confused by suggesting that MTPD is estimated as (at least) two time periods and a period of less than normal capacity, thus:

- the maximum time period after the start of a disruption within which the activity needs to be resumed,
- the minimum level at which the activity needs to be performed on its resumption,
- the length of time within which normal levels of operation need to be resumed

So it could be interpreted as either the point of initial resumption or the point at which normal operation is resumed. In practice this level of detail (particularly how the minimum level is to be described) is difficult to define and verify. In an initial BIA the complex parameters around phased recovery may not be understood until the analysis is complete. In addition, when writing and invoking plans, it complicates management of the recovery because the procedures necessary to make 'minimum levels' of resources operate effectively have to be carefully managed.

It is easier in practice to define this 'minimum level work' as a separate activity to the remaining 'normal work', since it must be different in its operation or time imperatives. If a more complex phased recovery needs to be planned it can be described by identifying further separate activities.

In this text it will be assumed that a product, service, process and activity has an MTPD and that an activity is either suspended or fully operational. If a phased recovery approach is to be used without defining the separate activities the same method can be used but the data collection and analysis, and subsequent maintenance, will be more complicated.

Alternative terms

There are other terms which sometimes mean the same thing as MTPD, one of which is 'maximum allowable outage' (MAO). However, 'allowable' is somewhat ambiguous (who is allowing it?) and 'outage' is

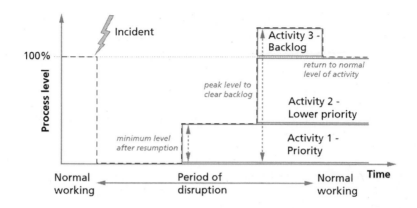

Figure 6   Phased process recovery described as separate activities

too easily equated with computer outages. In addition, a 'disruption' can include a service degradation or intermittent loss whereas 'outage' implies only complete stoppage. Other terms such as 'maximum acceptable downtime' (MAD) suffer from similar ambiguities.

MTPD of products and services

The MTPD of products and services is determined primarily by customer response. How long will the customer wait and what impacts will the failure to deliver have on the organization? This depends on many factors including:

- the availability of alternative sources
- competitor response
- pressure from your customer's customers
- contractual penalties
- reputational damage
- financial impacts
- regulatory requirements
- welfare and safety

Which of these factors is relevant and their nature depends on the specific products and services and the sector in which the organization operates. These impacts will be identified and the MTPD estimated in the Strategic BIA.

As stated in Chapter 1, section headed BIA scope, a 'product' or 'service' can be defined in various ways. It could be a group of products that share the same time imperatives, or it could be a single product delivered to a specific customer with the same product supplied to others being treated as a separate product. The terms can be used in whatever way seems to best fit the organization's analysis needs.

MTPD of activities

BS 25999-2 places a requirement to identify the MTPD of all activities (as well as products and services); this has been criticized as too onerous. The presumed alternative is to set a recovery time objective (RTO) (see later in this Chapter, section headed Recover time objective) during the BIA. However, the setting of RTOs requires a full understanding of activity interrelationships which will not be available until the BIA is complete. Therefore it is still useful to use the BIA to identify the MTPD of processes and activities within the context of the MTPD(s) of the products and services they support and to understand the reason behind this determination.

In general the MTPD of processes and front office activities is determined by the urgency of the products and services that they deliver.

The MTPD of the support activities is then determined by the urgency of the front-line activities they support. Sometimes this link may be relatively direct; others may be more convoluted.

ISO/DIS 22301 similarly specifies a requirement to prioritize activities, taking into consideration the time within which the impacts of not resuming the activities would become unacceptable and having understood their role in supporting the provision of products and services.

Understanding business activities

All business activities can be described as having inputs, a process and outputs. BCM is obviously interested in the inputs and outputs (since these are the interdependencies that have to be understood). Understanding the process itself is not usually a BCM requirement except for two aspects: its resource requirements (see section headed Types of resource, later in this chapter) and its duration.

For the purposes of BIA, business activities fall into two groups:

- Continuous – where the duration of the individual activities in a process is short, and so it can be treated as continuous. An example would be a customer help desk where most enquiries are answered within a few minutes and, after any interruption, the operation can be resumed once the cause of the disruption has been fixed.
- Periodic – where the time taken to produce the output is significant: days, weeks or even years. Periodic activities usually have delivery

deadlines (fixed by customer contracts or external requirements). Typical periodic activities in business include manufacturing, accounts and projects. Sometimes the process needs to be started again from scratch after an interruption where the work in progress cannot be salvaged. Examples of these are manufacturing processes and biological experiments which may take hours, days, months or even years from start to completion.

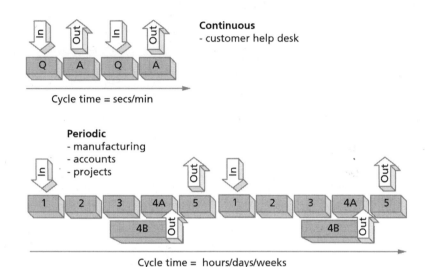

Figure 7   Different types of activity

For periodic activities the MTPD is a more complex concept and could apply to several time periods:

- from the start of the process to its latest required delivery time;
- from completion of the process to its latest required delivery time;
- for the maximum spare time between a set of processes;
- for how long the process can be stopped before it has to be restarted.

All of the above are acceptable uses of the concept within an organization but, because of this ambiguity, it is vital that it is clear which of the many interpretations is being employed.

Some specific examples of periodic activities are discussed in the next section.

Difficult disruption times

With some activities, the timing of the disruption makes a considerable difference to the impact experienced by the organization. Payroll is the activity most often quoted in this context. On the day of the payroll run, a few hours lost can result in unhappy staff and a complex sorting out of any personal financial problems caused by late payment. Yet once a monthly payroll run is completed, the activity can probably be disrupted for three weeks before its resumption becomes pressing.

Other common activities with periodicity of this nature include:

* daily, monthly and annual accounting and regulatory reporting;
* seasonal peaks and troughs, such as school holidays for travel operators;
* for a university the failure of the admissions procedures at student registrations could have implications on student numbers for several years afterwards;
* external reporting schedules, such as stock value reporting at a specific time each day;
* projects with a fixed implementation date;
* response – where an activity (such as IT support or building maintenance) is only required if something goes wrong.

The general rule for these is to assume that the incident could occur at the worst possible time relative to the deadline to be met (sometimes known as Murphy's Law).

Murphy's Law in action: The London Stock Exchange was closed for nearly eight hours by a computer failure on 5 April 2000 – the last day of the tax year.

Pragmatic and often individual solutions may need to be found for each of these challenges. Some questions that could be asked are:

* Is missing the deadline business-threatening or just embarrassing? How much embarrassment is tolerable?
* Could the deadline be extended in extenuating circumstances? This may require advance agreement with regulators or through special service level agreements with customers.
* Could the activity be performed sooner – for example, always running the payroll a day earlier would give more time to deal with any disruption?

- Are several projects being undertaken concurrently? Can they all be treated in the BIA as one continuous activity, or does each project require its own recovery plan?

Certain activities appear, at first, to be intolerant of any interruption. The implications of any outage are uncertain but could be catastrophic. Some examples are given below with some suggestions for contemplation. This is not guidance – only those responsible for the service can make the decision.

- Real-time share trading – here the issue is the potential loss or profit that might occur should the interruption prevent trading during a period of volatility. Since the potential impact is primarily financial, it may be appropriate for the business to make the decision on MTPD on the probability of the impact of the trading opportunities lost over various time periods. Despite the claimed intolerance to any interruption, most trading firms accept relocation recovery strategies that could entail a break of several hours.
- Banks spend significant sums on strategies to minimize the length of interruptions but several have experienced service problems lasting many hours, and in one case several days, without losing customers.
- Reporting of the financial position at a specific time each day (a regulatory requirement). When pressed it was agreed that a one- or even a two-day deadline could be missed provided a plan could be produced to show how the problem was being resolved.
- Emergency services control rooms – when the potential impact of a disruption is loss of a life that could have been saved it may be judged that only disruptions of seconds or a few minutes are acceptable. However, this loss is only potential; it is not certain that a delay would result in a loss of life at any particular instant.
- Air traffic control – a failure here would create an immediate threat to the safety of those airborne at that time.
- Life support – there is an immediate threat to life if these systems fail.

It appears that only the last two examples cannot tolerate any interruption. If an interruption of only a few seconds is acceptable then, fortunately, there are solutions that can take advantage of this tolerance to provide alternatives.

Agreeing the estimate of an MTPD is challenging in some circumstances but it is difficult to see any other way of justifying the appropriate solutions for provision of continuity. Even without full agreement, the discussion can prove useful in identifying further issues to explore which may then lead to a consensus.

MTPD of projects and events

In some organizations, projects and events form a significant part of the workload. In this case the BCM programme may need to consider them in the context of a disruption.

The nature of projects varies but, although most can survive some form of interruption, some may have to be delivered on a specific date with no delay being acceptable. Similarly, events may have some slack time in their preparation but have to run on the day. A late delivery means they may have to be cancelled entirely and the expense written off with no return.

There are several ways to deal with projects and events with a BIA:

- If they form a small part of the operation: leave projects and events out of the scope of the BIA.
- Where there are a number of small projects: treat projects as a single continuous activity where the priorities will be sorted out post-incident.
- For large or strategic projects: undertake a BIA on each project as part of the planning process.

None of the above solutions is ideal but the pragmatic solution may be dictated by the expected structure of the recovery plans and how they might deal with recovering projects – whether they would be recovered standalone or along with operational activities. The business recovery plan will certainly need to have an early step that reassesses recovery time objectives after the incident, and this will need to include a review of projects and events.

Recovery time objective

In the BCI's *GPG 2010* and BS 25999-1, the parameter 'recovery time objective' (RTO) does not appear in the section on BIA: instead it appears as one of the first steps in determining the recovery strategies. This is logical since setting an objective is a decision rather than part of a process of understanding. However, it does appear in the requirements of the BIA section of BS 25999-2 and in ISO/DIS 22301. For consistency a discussion of the term is left to Chapter 7, section headed Recovery time objective, where it is shown how the BIA data is used to set the RTO prior to selecting BCM strategies.

Is the activity 'critical'?

The word 'critical' has caused more confusion within the BCM field than any other. It seems to have first been used originally to describe the equipment considered essential at a disaster recovery site. As initial BIAs were often IT-led, it became common to describe a step in the BCM process **before** the BIA where management identified 'critical functions' or 'critical business functions' to describe the scope of the BIA. There was no guidance given on what constituted a 'critical' or 'non-critical' function; managers were expected to know. Some methods suggest the classification of activities into 'critical, essential, necessary or desirable'. Some texts, finding critical too weak, use 'mission critical' and one even added 'super critical' to the list! Perhaps 'hyper critical' will come next.

As the BIA became more business focused it then became clear that it was the BIA itself that should define what was 'critical' to the organization on the basis of the impact that a disruption would cause. So in BS 25999-1 it is described as a separate step **after** the BIA, with the following guidance allowing organizations to focus its planning only on 'critical activities'.

Dictionary definitions of 'critical' use words such as 'important' and 'indispensable'. How do these then differ from 'essential' and 'necessary' in the classification above? And if the activity is 'unimportant' or 'dispensable', why is it being done at all?

> A small voluntary organization, distributing grants to local enterprises, noted each of their interactions with stakeholders (i.e. services) on cards and then, after some discussion, reorganized the cards according to urgency. Interestingly the final order was almost the exact reverse of the order in which they had identified each service, because initially they had been guided by their perception of the 'importance' of each service rather than its urgency.

> The reason for the confusion is that the word 'critical' lacks a **time** parameter – what we could say is that an activity becomes 'critical' at a certain time. However, because this distinction is rarely made, those questioned about the 'criticality' of an activity for which they are responsible assume the question to mean 'How **important** is your activity?'. The answer to the question, of course, is 'very important' because it is their job and identifies their position in the organization even if the activity it is not very time sensitive!

The result is that, when setting the priorities for the resumption of activity, decisions are frequently made based on (perceived) importance rather than its real time imperative. The resulting recovery requirements often show an urgency of resumption which is actually unnecessary. Moreover, individuals may see a threat to their jobs or standing in the organization if they are labelled as 'non-critical' and will, in consequence, exaggerate their role: this is often the case with more senior staff.

> Asking a manager if an activity was 'critical' received the response that 'someone asked me that question last week'. The manager was confusing a BIA enquiry with an efficiency consultant who had been touring the business looking for potential redundancies. It is worrying that a BIA can be so misunderstood by using ambiguous jargon.

As to alternative terms, the obvious one is the word 'urgent'; it is clear and unambiguous about timescale. Another alternative is 'priority'. More clumsy is the term 'time-critical', though this may be an easier term to employ where 'critical' is entrenched. It should be accepted in a BIA that everything an organization does is important, but not everything is urgent.

It is now, therefore, generally accepted that the role of the BIA is to establish the urgency of each of its products, services and activities – not to try to judge their 'importance', whatever that means. Dividing our staff into 'critical' and 'non-critical' is divisive and may threaten our recovery if we ignore the 'non-critical' staff who, after an incident, may find other employment as they are not expecting to be recalled to work.

What the use of the term 'critical activities' is trying to imply is that we do not write detailed plans for areas of the business that do not need to be resumed for several weeks following a disruption. So, as a guide, the more urgent the activity is, the more detailed the plans need to be and the availability of recovery resources after an incident needs to have more certainty.

This confusion may be coming to an end as standards developed by ASIS/BSI (BCM.01 2010) and ISO/DIS 22301 are no longer using 'critical'; instead the BIA sets 'prioritized timeframes' for resuming activities. These standards also require that each activity has a level of recovery capability and detail of planning appropriate to its priority.

Maximum tolerable data loss (MTDL)

An incident may lead to the loss of data by damage or denial of access to the equipment that either holds or can access the live information. In this event the data, if required, needs to be accessed from an alternate source. This could be a 'mirrored' copy of the data, a tape in an off-site store, or paper records (such as purchase orders).

This poses two issues to recovering activities that rely on data for their operation:

- the time it takes to recover access to the data (which must be less than the MTPD);
- the currency of the data; if the recovered data is too out of date, it may hamper the operation of the activity and prolong the disruption beyond the tolerable period.

This issue is not confined to electronic data but any form of information that is not duplicated at an off-site location, such as working papers, cheques, customer orders or scientific experiments. It is therefore useful to address the topic with each manager in order to identify potential issues to address later.

Maximum survivable incident

When undertaking a BIA you need to have a context that describes the assumptions you are making. Many of these assumptions relate to scales of distance and incident intensity. These should be stated in the BCM policy and influence the strategy but, for the moment, are working assumptions. Unfortunately the language to describe these assumptions is not well developed. An example will make this clearer.

Suppose an organization has two sites in one country and one in another, each self-contained and all producing the same service to their 'local' customers. An incident could affect:

1. one site – caused by, for example, a fire or localized event;
2. two sites – a strike in the country with two sites;
3. all three – if a supplier to all three sites failed;
4. all three plus their customers – in the event of widespread bad weather or a pandemic;
5. a devastating, widespread event across the whole area, such as a major earthquake or war.

In the BIA we will ask the question: 'How long will our customers tolerate not receiving the service?'. The answer may be the same in the first three circumstances, but the organization's ability to cope with the situation, the number of customers affected and the potential reputational impacts are very different. In the fourth situation the customer may not be in a position to receive the service so a substantial delay may be acceptable, and in the last scenario the whole environment in which the organization operates has changed and its continuance may be impossible or irrelevant.

With the exception of the response agencies, organizations do not plan for the last, the 'worst-case' or 'Armageddon', situation because recovering the organization (at least in its current form) is inappropriate and probably impossible. The bad weather, pandemic and other widespread situations provide so many imponderables in their effect on supply chains and infrastructure that this should not be considered by an initial BIA, although it may be examined, perhaps with an exercise, later. Widespread disruptions may not threaten an organization as rapidly because everyone is affected and so there are lower expectations. However, there may be an opportunity to be gained if the organization is better prepared than its competitors.

> When the volcano Eyjafjallajokull caused havoc to airline freight and passengers across Europe, a worldwide logistics company was able to pick up substantial extra business from competitors because its transport fleet was more diverse, allowing it to divert traffic onto ship and road under its own control rather than through subcontractors.

It is the localized incidents that provide the greater challenge since others in the same sector are unaffected by the disruption, so attention is focused on the organization's troubles. So, to return to the situation list above, one of the smaller scale situations – a site, countrywide or organization-wide failure – should be used as the geographical scope. Which of these to choose may depend, in part, on the degree of self-sufficiency of the sites. It is suggested that the default should be to consider a single site disruption situation in the initial BIA with the BCM strategy stage looking at the feasibility of using the other sites for continuity. As the BCM programme matures, the wider issues of multiple site failures can be explored.

> A reinsurance firm located in the centre of a city's financial district recognized that small localized incidents were of greater concern than a widespread incident, which would also disrupt their competitors who were all located close by.

Similar arguments can be applied to the scale of staff loss. If large numbers of staff are unavailable there is a point where the operation of the organization becomes unviable (because of operational or safety implications, for example) and if the loss of staff is as a result of death or serious injury caused by the organization's own negligence, its reputation may be irreparable and closure is then inevitable.

It is this idea of scale and intensity that the term 'maximum survivable incident' tries to convey (though it is not in common use). It is good practice to spell out the limits and assumptions of the BCM response, either in the BCM policy or in a BCM strategy document. This will make top management aware of the limitations of the situations that have been planned for and beyond which they may need to make some difficult decisions.

Resources

This part of the BIA is sometimes separately identified as a 'continuity requirements analysis'. Its purpose is to identify and quantify the resources required to undertake each activity. These may include people, premises, technology, information and suppliers. If the resource information is available from the same sources as the timescale requirement, this information can be collected at the same time.

If the Strategic, Tactical and Operational model of undertaking the BIA process is being used (see Chapters 4, 5 and 6), the detailed resource information will be collected at the lowest (operational) level allowing the tactical analysis to focus on the issues of recovery timing. There is more detail on the information to be collected in the Operational BIA, which is described in Chapter 6.

Types of resource

The resources required for activities may consist of:

Staff

This could just be a number of staff, but could also include a requirement for particular skills or qualifications since this may affect the choice of recovery strategies. For simplicity use 'full-time equivalents' where there are part-time staff, to avoid double counting.

Additional staff may be required (see the following sections) to make workarounds effective and to clear backlogs within a tolerable time period.

Premises

For office-based activities this may simply be a number of desks. For others it may be defined in terms of space (mail sorting room) or function (aircraft hanger).

Technology and equipment

Office activities may define resource requirements such as desktop equipment (PCs, dealing desks); others may require specific machinery or other equipment. Shared equipment, such as printers and photocopiers, may need to be taken into account. The requirement for special equipment (printers for cheque signatures, special software) should be particularly noted, whereas data collection can be simplified by assuming the need for a default desktop configuration with only the exceptions noted.

Information

Information may be required from computer applications, paper records, reference information or other sources to enable the activity to be undertaken.

Unless decided otherwise each set of data will need to be available before the MTPD of the activity that requires it. Therefore a key output is a list of computer applications that will define the detailed requirements of the IT recovery priorities.

The required currency (see section headed MTDL earlier in this chapter) of modifiable electronic and other data should also be defined. This can be used to define the back-up and restoration strategy in the event of loss of records.

Supplies

Some activities require external supplies, such as raw materials, to operate. The time parameters should be investigated; these may include contracted service levels, procurement processes, alternative suppliers and safety stocks held.

Some operational requirements are common to all or most activities – such as electricity and the organization's standard desktop configuration. To minimize the information collected, it is suggested that they are left out of the data collection entirely (their urgency is that of the most urgent activity) but should be further considered when devising BCM strategy.

Workarounds

A workaround is a procedure developed by a department or business process to cope with the temporary loss of a particular resource. For example:

- manual processing if IT systems are not available;
- delaying filing or processing of paperwork if there is a staff shortage.

The existence and practicality of workarounds are useful topics to explore during a BIA since they can differentiate the urgency and resource requirements of various activities and they may later form part of a recovery strategy. However, they tend to be useful only for a short period, may require additional resources to operate or clear the resulting backlogs and tend not to work unless regularly used.

Although they have the potential to extend the MTPD by allowing the activity to continue for a longer period, in practice it is usually safer to disregard them at this stage but to incorporate them into activity recovery plans as options. They should never be used as a reason to leave an activity out of the BIA on the grounds that 'it is already covered'.

The CEO's office kept the CEO's diary online. One morning the staff came in to find the system was unavailable, so were unable to inform the CEO of his appointments. Now they print off a rolling one-week diary each evening and the PA takes it home, so even if there is a denial of access, the CEO's appointments can be managed.

Backlogs

The assumption is often made that a business activity can be resumed immediately once the IT systems and other required resources are available. It is also often assumed that an activity can be resumed with fewer resources than usual, with staff concentrating on certain tasks. However, there are many reasons that can delay the return of an activity to normal and require the availability of more, rather than fewer, resources than normal.

- Delays to product delivery may create a demand from customers for extra supplies once production is restored.

- Similarly because the activity has not been operational for a while, it may have to operate at a higher level temporarily to meet customer demand.
- Data created since the last secured back-up may have been lost, and this data may have to be recreated in whole or part before the activity can be resumed.
- The activity may have been run manually while awaiting the restoration of systems. The data produced from this temporary method may need to be added before the activity can return to normal.

For all of these reasons there may be a period of time in which additional resources are required by the activity; otherwise the disruption will be prolonged intolerably.

The definition of MTPD does not specify whether the time period should be measured to the point at which the activity is first resumed or the point at which the back-log is cleared and normal process resumed. In practice this will not usually significantly affect the estimation of MTPD at the tactical level but becomes more significant when working on the detail of activity recovery at the operational level.

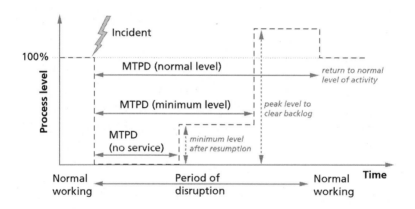

Figure 8   Various interpretations of MTPD

Interdependencies

The interdependencies of an organization's activities and dependence on external suppliers create significant difficulties when recovering a business after a disruption. It is therefore vital that these interrelationships are understood in the BIA.

There may be many complex processes involving more than one department within a business. A typical internal relationship is the coordination of tasks undertaken by goods-in, procurement, accounts and the receiving department to ensure ordering, receipt and payment of the supplier. It may be appropriate to define this as one 'process' for the purpose of a Tactical BIA, leaving the individual components to be analysed as activities at the operational level.

External dependencies may include:

- the supply of raw materials or consumables;
- incoming and outgoing communications (mail, telephony or e-mail);
- information from a source;
- delivery of goods to a customer;
- services provided to a customer on your behalf;
- maintenance and support services provided by third parties.

The relationship with some stakeholders may have both customer and supplier elements. These may include:

- partners;
- regulators;
- Group head office and other Group companies.

Dependence on IT

To judge by adverts for IT data storage and back-up technology, every organization requires instant and unfailing access to its applications, and they claim this is becoming more pressing, as if that were possible, every day. This appears to make the BIA redundant, at least with regard to the ICT requirements of the BCM strategy, since instant IT availability appears to be a given.

However, in the event of IT staff being unavailable, applications rarely stop functioning immediately. Similarly, the failure of an item of IT equipment may cause a degradation of service rather than a complete failure. Instead there is a gradual decline of quality and security as machine and application failures are not fixed, back-ups are not taken and patches not applied. This makes it difficult to generalize the urgency of IT as a single 'activity'.

MTPD of IT

Although it may not be a popular stance to take with some IT departments, all BCM resource requirements (IT applications, staff, accommodation, etc.) are only as urgent as the activities which those resources support. In addition, workarounds may make it possible for the activity to function for a short time without IT. Therefore, from the perspective of IT (as with other resource providers), the role of the BIA is to create a requirements definition that identifies when each application is required during the recovery process. In theory IT can just take the application list with MTPDs and MTDLs to design and implement their disaster recovery strategy with appropriate back-up and restore capabilities.

In practice the situation is more complex:

- Activity requirements after an incident may differ from those used during normal operations.
- If the incident causes operational disruption as well as IT loss then IT recovery priorities may be different from those applicable to a disruption caused by an IT failure alone.
- The IT department itself may have activities that need to be prioritized, such as development projects to meet deadlines or those that have had substantial investment.
- IT may already have made significant investment in DR facilities, which the BIA might prove not to have been required.

Activity requirements

Activities may be able to cope without certain IT systems for a while, but this may create backlogs of work which then have to be dealt with. Clearing those backlogs may require extra IT capacity beyond normal requirements; and they will not be cleared if the extra demand slows system response.

For customer-facing activities and for managing the disruption, the telephone is often seen as being required before IT. However, the increasing convergence of telephony and IT with Voice over IP (VoIP) and call centre applications has blurred this distinction.

IT failures and priorities

The priorities that are apparent to the IT department during a disruption resulting from an IT failure are usually different from those during an incident involving facilities damage. The priorities during an IT failure (which are usually perceived as more likely) may reflect internal needs, rather than those relating directly to services to customers. IT's strategy may be to maintain high availability of particular IT systems, but these may not be the same systems that require the recovery priority after a major incident.

A logistics firm suffered a 12-hour outage as a result of a hard disk crash on the distribution server, which took the business several weeks to recover from because of its impact on deliveries, invoicing and debt collection. Most of its IT equipment was in a data centre but one substantial server, which ran a marketing system, was housed at head office 50 km away.

The IT manager wanted to move the marketing server to the data centre and link it to the distribution system server to create a high availability cluster and asked for support for this proposal on the basis of reducing the likelihood of another distribution system failure.

Whilst the likelihood of system failure before and after the creation of the cluster might be estimated from previous experiences, there were, of course, no reliable probability estimates for the loss of the data centre because of the infinite number of threats. One threat, however, was highly visible since the data centre was directly under the flight path of a nearby major airport.

A Tactical BIA demonstrated that the marketing server's loss could be tolerated for weeks. However, it had a second role as the DR machine for the distribution system if the data centre was damaged where it could be quickly reconfigured in a standby location at the head office.

The MTPD of the distribution system was obviously more than 12 hours but the impact of the incident it had experienced led to the conclusion that it was just a few days because:

- the interruption to cashflow would quickly cause a problem as a result of recent high borrowing to fund capital works;

and

- though much of the distribution was regular contract work, it is a very competitive market so customers could quickly move to other logistics providers to protect their own customers.

> If the distribution server was damaged, the rapid recovery of
> the distribution application relied on the immediate availability
> of the marketing server at the other site. Therefore, in the
> absence of an alternative IT DR strategy, the recommendation
> to move the marketing server to the data centre was not
> supported by the BIA since recovery of the distribution system
> could take several weeks if new equipment needed to be
> purchased and configured.

IT activities

Some activities can be identified as having an MTPD because of the
dependencies that other activities have on them, such as the IT help desk.

Major IT development projects may also have an MTPD where they are
required to meet a contractual, statutory or regulatory obligation. If the
project is absorbing a significant amount of effort or expenditure there
may be an impact on share prices if there is a delay in implementation,
and thus an MTPD could be estimated – but is likely to be measured in
weeks or months.

Existing disaster recovery provision

The organization may have some existing IT DR provision in place,
although examining the capabilities of existing DR provision is best left
until the strategy stage where they can be compared against the
requirements that come out of the BIA. The capabilities of existing DR
provision therefore form useful background information, but are not
essential to the BIA itself.

IT service companies

Few of the above comments apply to an IT service company whose
products and services are providing access applications, support and
development directly to customers; the external IT function thus becomes
the 'front office' in the BIA.

Some organizations have attempted to treat their IT departments as a
separate IT service company in a BIA. This is not really effective since the
impacts of a disruption fall on the whole organization, not just the IT
department.

An IT services company took recovery of its customer's data very seriously and frequently visited a third party site to undertake recovery tests. The BIA identified the recovery of the Customer Helpdesk to be far more urgent than the systems themselves since customers' need for information was the first priority.

BIA in different sectors

BIA in a manufacturing environment

In some respects the BIA method is easier to apply in a manufacturing environment since there is a tangible product delivered to one or more customers, often under a contract. So, at a strategic level, it should be relatively easy to determine an MTPD for each product.

However, the supply chain may add a layer of complexity where products are held and distributed to customers by agents or wholesalers; this may make the identification of the 'customer' and the estimation of the MTPD for products and services more difficult.

Some manufacturing processes involve many raw materials and assembly steps. It is easy to become absorbed in the detail of the various steps and there will be many potential causes of disruptions embedded there. Again, it is important to retain focus on the purpose of the BIA, which is to identify the parameters of appropriate recovery strategies at each level.

At the strategic level the focus should be on the likely response of customers to a disruption, so contracts and knowledge about competitors will be the main sources of information. A view should be taken as to whether a disruption that might be tolerable within a current contract may jeopardize renewal of the contract or future contracts. This research may need to understand the potential impacts and timescales throughout the downstream supply chain.

There are a limited number of options for activity recovery in the manufacturing sector (compared to those for office relocation). Possible solutions for continuity include:

- subcontracting part or all of the processes to one or more other manufacturers, even if they are competitors, since that is otherwise where your customers will go;
- using other production facilities within the company;
- contracts for providing rapid replacement equipment from plant manufacturers;
- alternative or temporary buildings;

- off-site warehousing of finished products.

A company manufactured a component for several car assembly companies. For some customers a few generic components were supplied (so could be held in stock); for others each component was individually customized and was manufactured and delivered to a schedule within a day. The car could not be completed without this component so the production line would have to stop if it was not available. However, the customer was unable to change quickly to another supplier during a disruption as the set-up time for another supplier to make exactly the same product would be several months.

The company was part of a group with a similar plant in another European country. One customer was placing a BCM requirement on its key suppliers but was also insisting that supplier costs were kept low and declining year on year.

In the Strategic BIA it was decided to differentiate between the customized product and the standard products, but not to distinguish between the supply to different customers. However, in practice there was felt to be little difference between their MTPDs, though tactically there were considerable differences in recovering the processes.

The estimation of an MTPD of several days took into account:

- the reputational impact of a supply disruption, which could lose future orders;
- the lack of immediate alternative supplies for the products;
- the financial impact of disruption, which could be mitigated by business interruption insurance.

The Tactical BIA identified the steps in the process which included:

- aluminium casting, moulding, customization, warehousing and distribution; these processes took only a few hours to perform so were not individually examined;
- reliance on moulds from a subcontractor situated on the same site – which had a lead time of many months to produce.

The strategy devised to meet these requirements included:

- storing spare moulds off-site;
- moving production to the Group's other plant using air freight for products in the first instance;

> - using subcontractors to undertake finishing and testing processes;
> - cancelling the DR contract on the accounts computer, the loss of which could be coped with for several weeks since customer payments were made on delivery without invoicing.

Restoring production may be hampered by long lead times and the specialist nature of production equipment. Finding alternative production facilities may be subject to limited availability as the plant is usually heavily utilized. Transport to enable alternative locations to be used may involve complex logistics (in respect of both raw materials and product), significant time and substantial costs.

> A company manufactured credit cards for several banks. For one bank alternative facilities were found in another country and relocation rehearsed on small print runs. However, running all work at the alternative site would have to be scheduled overnight and at weekends. Various issues required resolution once the technical issues had been resolved; these included:
>
> - regulatory agreement for transmitting customer data to and printing cards in another financial jurisdiction;
> - regional labour regulations that limited staff working hours, so overtime and weekend work by local staff would not be possible;
> - national transport regulations which prohibited trucking of the cards on Sundays.

As a result, the Operational BIA may have to look carefully both at the time imperatives and detailed technical requirements of the processes and logistics if it is to provide sufficient information for appropriate strategies to be selected.

BIA in government and public bodies

Undertaking a BIA in a government or other public body creates many challenges in terms of scope. Government agencies often have a very wide range of responsibilities, sometimes with little in common, yet a BIA needs to find a common acceptance of priorities.

The issue of who is the 'customer' was discussed in an earlier section (see section headed Defining the 'customer', earlier in this chapter). In some cases the receiver of the service is fairly obvious but in others, such as a corporate department setting policy, it is more difficult to identify. Although the public or electorate is the final customer of most government services, it may be more productive to see their elected representative as the customer who is accountable to them for the service and who can then make, or at least endorse, decisions on recovery timescales. It is not necessarily an easy task to gain commitment to these decisions.

In some cases it is difficult to clearly identify even a product or service delivered by departments focusing on strategic issues, although in this case the activities are unlikely to require rapid recovery and will therefore not require detailed analysis.

One place to start is the 'statutory duties' of the organization. This should identify a number of obligated 'services' which the body has to perform, though there is rarely a time limit placed on their delivery in the legislation. It is possible that they are audited on their performance of these duties and, if so, audit reports provide useful background to their requirements.

Other duties are discretionary but may result in a number of impacts if not delivered. These may include (with examples):

- political repercussions (social services);
- public safety and welfare issues (emergency response capabilities);
- compensation claims (planning delays);
- reputation damage to the agency (promised services or improvement not delivered).

The criterion for identifying a maximum tolerable period of disruption for a service is when this could lead to organizational failure. It needs to be appreciated that a public body can fail, albeit in a way that is different from a commercial failure. The difference is that the services of the public body will continue to be required, so it will need to operate after the disruption. Agency failure may therefore be evident when the name of the agency is changed and its senior management is replaced.

BIA in an emergency response organization

Emergency response organizations pose two problems specific to their role:

- They are expected to continue to operate in conditions more extreme than those which would have closed most other organizations.

- Their response times are expected to be immediate.

The 'maximum survivable incident' for these organizations will be of greater intensity than for those in the commercial sector. On the other hand the extent of their responsibility is often limited to a specific geographic area which clarifies this aspect of scope.

For these organizations, attempting to detail the various front line activities which may be called upon and their required speed of response is not a useful exercise since these priorities will be assigned dynamically according to the circumstances at the time. But a generic list, as in the example in the case study below, can provide a useful context for determining the MTPDs of the various supporting activities.

This context is vital as those managing emergency organizations, by the nature of their response mindset, often require to be convinced of the need for effective and timely recovery of their supporting activities.

> A police force came up (after an exercise-style BIA) with the following list of 'services' to the public and other organizations:
>
> - handling emergency calls
> - command and control
> - managing major incidents
> - maintaining public order
> - maintaining traffic management
> - recording and investigating crime
> - maintaining community liaison
> - maintaining CJS processes
> - handling non-emergency calls
> - maintaining administrative processes
>
> The list is in the agreed priority order, with the less urgent services being able to be delayed for hours and, in some cases, days.

BIA in an organization with distributed outlets

It is difficult to give general guidance as to how to scope the BIA process for organizations where there are many points of delivery to the customer – such as retail, networks and utilities.

The chosen structure may depend on many factors, including the ease with which the service can be delivered from another facility.

For example, a multinational retailer with many sales outlets:

- may not involve BCM in looking at the impact of a disruption to one brand of a product as this is a day-to-day operational issue;
- may be able to tolerate the loss of business from one outlet indefinitely, so a BIA for each outlet may not be required;
- within each country/region will probably want to undertake a BIA for each of its distribution centres since it is likely each will need a recovery plan because of the substantial loss of customers from stores that would result from lack of stock. A decision would need to be made, based on how similar they are, as to whether the conclusions from one distribution centre could be generalized to all the others;
- should undertake a BIA for its national and international head office functions.

In this example it is apparent that many of the strategic decisions (on product delivery) are likely to be made at the distribution centre level whereas much of the head office operation will be supporting activities.

The guidance could be applied, admittedly with more difficulty, to similar hierarchies such as telecommunications and utility networks. For example, within a rail network the focus may be on the operation of the control centres and rolling stock maintenance facilities, rather than on the track itself.

It is apparent that in a complex organization considerable thought is needed as to how to structure both the BIA programme and the BCM response structure.

Alternative approaches

This section looks at some alternative approaches to the BIA process that can be chosen by, or maybe forced upon, the organization by circumstances, and includes an indication of their possible shortcomings.

How does risk fit into a BIA?

The short answer is – it doesn't.

In the BIA we are identifying the timescales of recovery of our product and service delivery imposed on us by our customers, who will tolerate only so much delay to the promises we have made. There is no element of probability in that assessment: they will definitely go elsewhere if we fail to satisfy them within their tolerable time.

As BCM is seen by many organizations as being closely aligned with Risk Management, it is perhaps strange that there is no mention of impact analysis in ISO 31000, *Risk management — Principles and guidelines*, nor of business continuity.

A risk approach to BIA

The Australian/New Zealand Business Continuity standard AS/NZS 5050 takes the view that BCM is just a subset of Risk Management and defines a BIA as a:

> detailed risk analysis that examines the nature and extent of disruptions and the likelihood of the resulting consequences

and explains in a Note that it

> may (sic) include consideration of the organization's business functions, people, processes, infrastructure, resources, information, interdependencies and the nature and extent of capability loss over time

This is not a BIA definition that is consistent with any other national or international BCM standard or guidance. Given the unpredictable and unexpected nature of many disruptions, attempting to base a BCM strategy on predicted threats with speculative probability statistics appears perverse. As a result this approach does not provide the coherent and replicable results necessary to select appropriate continuity options. There is no useful purpose in confusing the clarity of the BIA with a multiplicity of incident causes and probability.

This discrepancy of method may create difficulties for multinational organizations that have to operate in this area and are expected to adopt local standards.

The order of BIA and risk analysis

The order in which risk analysis and BIA should be conducted in a BCM programme has been a long-running discussion in the BCM profession. The Business Continuity Institute (www.thebci.org) makes its belief plain in the *GPG 2010* which states:

> A BIA should be completed in advance (of a Risk Assessment) to identify the organization's most urgent activities.

However the first three Professional Practices in the DRII's list (www.drii.org) are:

1. Project Initiation and Management

2.   Risk Analysis and Control
3.   Business Impact Analysis

While the introductory section says that the sections are not presented in any sequence, it is usually assumed from their order that a risk analysis should precede the BIA – implying that the BIA should only be undertaken with reference to the significant risks identified. As suggested above, natural phenomena and man-made catastrophes do not respect the limitations of our imagination nor follow a neat mathematical formula. The result may be that the BCM and BIA scope is limited to situations (such as 'we are unlikely to lose both of our adjacent buildings') which could be exceeded by an incident. The BCM response derived from these assumptions will then be unable to provide a solution.

It may be appropriate to undertake some mitigation measures on obvious threats and hazards, but these should not be at the expense of the recovery capability. It is much easier to obtain support and substantial funding for an apparently well-defined risk mitigation measure than a complete BCM programme but, as the author Nassim Taleb asserts in *The Black Swan*:

> 'We can't get much better at predicting. But we can get better at realizing how bad we are at predicting.'

and Terry Pratchett in *The Light Fantastic* asserts:

> 'Million-to-one chances crop up nine times out of ten.'

> However we will spot obvious threats when conducting a BIA and these should be identified and prioritized for action according to the urgency of the activity to which they relate rather than on the (guessed) probability of their occurrence.

Although the theoretical basis for risk analysis, when applied to major disruptions, is unsound, there is still a widespread acceptance at senior management level of its usefulness. If support for undertaking a BIA is lacking this might be changed by delivering a 'risk analysis' to the senior management which shows a significant risk of serious disruptions from a variety of sources – there seems to be little risk of comeback since it is an entirely subjective assessment.

Group structure

There is one area where a high-level risk analysis may precede a BCM programme. Where a Group company owns a number of subsidiaries, a risk analysis may be used to determine how important each subsidiary is to the Group's overall viability – and therefore which subsidiaries should be encouraged (and funded) to develop a BCM capability. Of course, the management of each subsidary may take a different view as they may have a different perspective.

> A European printing company, part of a multinational corporation, was testing its plans with a scenario exercise. The situation was being handled in an apparently successful way but the exercise was brought to an abrupt halt by an observer – a US executive from Group head office: 'By now you would have become such an embarrassment we would have shut you down'. The Group headquarters had not been involved in the BCM programme up to that point.

Quick BIAs

There are occasions when a formal Strategic BIA with top management is not practical or may not elicit the required information. In this case alternative means must be found. The following examples may suggest other ideas for identifying the key products and services and an estimate of MTPD.

> During an exercise with senior operational and support police staff, the key deliverables of the various services undertaken by the police were identified (from a provisional list drawn up beforehand). The urgency of each was assessed in the context of two quite different exercise scenarios. The first, a wide area power cut, identified the immediate concerns of the operational officers. The second scenario, a staff shortage incident, looked at activities that would cause problems, particularly to the support staff, within a few days.

> Local authorities are often responsible for a wide range of
> diverse services. The opening of a presentation to middle
> managers on BCM started with the announcement of a
> (fictitious) food poisoning incident affecting staffing at the
> offices. Following some background to the subject, this was
> followed up by a message purporting to come from the Chief
> Executive, requesting the managers at the presentation to
> prioritize their workloads for the next few days because of high
> staff absence. This enabled a provisional list of more urgent
> and less urgent activities to be agreed.

The findings of a 'quick' BIA can be of considerable value and may set
useful strategic priorities, but they rarely provide sufficient detail to
enable appropriate strategies to be selected. They may prove to be a
useful stimulus to participants to undertake further, more detailed, work.

Too much change?

Frequently used excuses to delay a BIA are claiming that everyone is too
busy, or that too much is changing at the moment.

Unfortunately incidents are no respecter of busy schedules and, if staff
are too busy doing their jobs in normal circumstances, this indicates that
there would be significant problems in recovering from a disruption
when there are backlogs to clear.

Change in an organization is both a concern and an opportunity. There
are often more things that can go wrong when change occurs, and less
experience of managing the consequences. At the same time, a BCM
input into the change process through a forward looking BIA may enable
measures to improve resilience to be implemented – such as splitting
urgent processes across two locations or creating potential recovery space
by networking meeting areas.

The types of planned change which should trigger a BIA revision include:

- a new product or production method;
- a relocation of business activities;
- organizational structure change, including staffing levels;
- a new supplier or outsourcing contract.

Nonetheless it is pointless proceeding with a BIA if the organization is in
upheaval, since it will be impossible to define a stable structure with
which to describe its processes and activities. It may also be pointless if

the environment in which the organization operates is undergoing significant and uncertain change, a situation that is sometimes experienced by public sector organizations after policy changes are announced but before the details of their implementation are finalized.

Can we 'fast-track' (by-pass) the BIA?

There can be a concern that the organization is left exposed whilst the BIA is in progress. The suggestion is to put some strategies in place and prepare some plans to protect the organization. Once complete, if required a BIA can then be undertaken to ensure that the strategies and plans were appropriate. Though this seems reasonable on the surface, it is difficult to see how a post-implementation BIA's findings would not support the strategy that had been implemented (even if it proved otherwise). Nor is it true that the organization is exposed during this period – a challenging BIA interview can make managers think, and start to plan before the formal planning process begins.

> An incident required partial relocation by an organization that was in the process of undertaking its first BIA. Most things went relatively smoothly because the BIA interviews had clarified the priorities and recovery requirements, even though plans had not been documented.

That said, there are a number of impact mitigation 'strategies' that should be put in place as soon as possible since they are obvious requirements, but are not dependent on the outcome of the BIA. These items, sometimes called 'quick wins', include:

- delivering a draft incident and media management plan (or checklist card) for the top management;
- forming an emergency response team;
- collating and testing a staff call-tree;
- setting up an emergency helpline for staff.

3 Planning the BIA – Project or Process?

The description of the BIA in texts and standards makes it appear that a BIA is a single project undertaken on a periodic basis.

When an organization is embarking on a BCM programme for the first time, a single BIA covering the whole organization can be a very useful tool in:

- deciding on the scope of the BCM programme;
- giving top management a feel for how the organization can implement BCM;
- identifying some 'quick wins' that can provide immediate capability within the organization.

However, the effort and cost of undertaking this annually can be a serious deterrent to repeating the exercise. Therefore, as the BCM programme develops, it may be more appropriate to view the BIA as a continuous process – a series of tasks at different levels that, over time, ensure that the BIA stays current to both organizational objectives and operational practices.

This chapter considers the planning issues of these two approaches.

BIA as a project

An organization's first attempt to undertake a BIA is likely to take place with a lack of clarity as to how the BCM programme will eventually be implemented and with limited in-house experience.

Sponsorship

The support of top management is, of course, essential for an effective BIA to be undertaken. It may therefore be necessary to undertake some form of awareness event with the executives so that they understand what is to be done, what is required of them, what can be expected to emerge and what it might lead to when complete.

Ideally one executive will be assigned as project sponsor and with this support, if only expressed by a signature on an email, doors will be opened, appointments kept and answers given. Expect to reciprocate this support with regular progress reports and meetings. Points of protocol, areas of disagreement and organizational strategy can be discussed at this meeting. It may be that significant developments are planned at executive level but have not yet been announced – and may make a difference to the results of the BIA. In this event it is vital to maintain the confidentiality of any information shared within the agreed limits.

Setting the initial terms of reference

While formal terms of reference can be agreed with the project sponsor, it is advisable to keep these open – or continuously negotiable. Trying to understand an organization, particularly for the first time, may throw up surprises that need to be investigated.

Products and services

Although the agreement of a BCM policy should be the initiator of a BCM programme, it is possible that a BIA is attempted before this is in place or finalized. In this case, the BIA may be used to identify appropriate groups of products and services. It can also be used to educate the decision as to which of these should be included or excluded from the programme scope.

> While looking at the incoming phone call volumes for a life insurance company's call centre, one extension received many more calls than others. Although the firm sold life insurance, one of its employees was an expert on other sorts of domestic insurance. With the full support of his manager, this person provided advice to independent financial advisers on domestic insurance in the expectation that life insurance business would also be directed to the company. In effect, this became a small but significant additional service to include in the BIA.

While this process is formally described in Chapter 4 in relation to the Strategic BIA, it is usefully preceded by an exploratory tactical level BIA with the intention of getting to know the operation of the business before proposing a scheme to top management. In a large organization it is unlikely that the top management are fully aware of every detail of the operation of the business for which they are responsible.

> A national Cooperative bank provided banking services, via
> small subsidiaries, to a range of occupational groups – such as
> nurses, doctors, tradesmen and farmers. The farming subsidiary
> ran a seed and fertilizer depot to provide these to its
> customers. This service was added to the scope of the bank's
> BCM programme.

Trial BIA

If time allows, even an experienced practitioner will find it useful to trial
run a BIA. This could take the form of a few interviews to try out a
response form or questionnaire with friendly colleagues who can
feedback on the questions.

The whole exercise can be undertaken initially with a limited scope of
one product or service. The experience gained will add significantly to
the confidence with which the wider project is tackled and the results
demonstrated may gain buy-in from colleagues to complete the whole
scope.

Duration and scope

Conventional project management methods suggest that the length of a
BIA can be determined by how much work is required. Other factors,
however, are crucial in planning what can be achieved.

The BIA is a snapshot of the organization's continuity requirements at a
point in time, so it becomes out of date as the business changes. A
protracted BIA in a fast-moving organization may be out of date before
it has been drafted and may require immediate revision.

The BIA is an ideal opportunity to make a case for BCM to managers.
However, the impetus that can be developed through face to face
interviews is transitory if no results are seen quickly.

Based on experience, from collecting the BIA data to drafting the report
should take no more than two months, so that rapid progress to
producing draft plans is apparent. Undertaking 'quick wins' – obvious
measures that do not require the confirmation of the BIA, such as
Communications Plans – can also help to maintain the momentum of the
BCM programme during the BIA project. If the project takes longer than
three months, it will probably be out of date before it is finished.

If this appears impossible, the scope of the BIA could be reduced to
fewer products and services, enabling progress to be demonstrated in this
limited scope first before tackling other areas of the business.

The optimum project team numbers

A BIA will not necessarily be completed more quickly by allocating more members to the project team. This is because one of the main outputs is an overview of the organization's operation and the interviews need to be conducted with consistency. A larger team will need to spend considerable time sharing their understanding with each other.

In practice, the ideal project team is two people, who should both attend all interviews: one to ask questions, the other to take notes. One of these may be an outside specialist (see the next section). Having only two people gives the advantage of consistency, and also the benefits of being able to share and discuss the results.

Again, if it proves impossible to cover the required scope with the resources available, the scope or level of detail should be reduced to enable the BIA to be completed within an acceptable time frame.

The role of external specialists

Many organizations successfully undertake the BIA process using only internal resources. There are advantages, however, in using an external qualified BIA specialist (holding certification such as Membership of the Business Continuity Institute) to assist on the first occasion because the independent consultant:

- will want to complete the task on time and within budget and, unlike internal resources, will not be diverted to other short-term tasks;
- is not likely to be influenced by internal politics;
- will be more able to challenge responses from senior management and technical specialists;
- will use their experience of other organizations to provide a reality check of the conclusions;
- may have more credibility with senior management than a member of staff.

There are downsides of using an external resource, most of which can be mitigated:

- External resources cost money – however, this may prove to be a good investment in reducing the time taken and improving the quality of the results.
- Skills and information will not be retained by the organization – internal staff should always attend each interview and be fully involved in the data analysis. Skills transfer should be a stated aim of any agreement with an external specialist.

- Confidentiality – this can be addressed through non-disclosure agreements.

It is not necessary to hire BCM specialists with particular knowledge of the sector; indeed, a new insight may be gained from a fresh approach.

Acquiring the skills

If a BIA is to be conducted using in-house resources it is essential that they have the appropriate expertise. While it is intended that this book should provide sufficient background and instruction on BIA methods, there are other skills which can prove useful.

Business

A good grasp of the business processes in the organization will save time during BIA interviews and give the confidence to challenge responses. This does not need to be a deep technical knowledge, but must be sufficient to demonstrate an understanding of the overall process and to enable challenging questions to be asked.

Each organization has its unique processes which will need to be explained, but knowledge of the following activities might be expected of interviewers:

- background to the sector in which the organization operates, including knowledge of the major customers;
- an outline knowledge of the organization's processes;
- accounts – processes for invoicing, payment of suppliers, general ledger and financial reporting;
- procurement – approval of suppliers, order placing, goods receipt and links with accounts;
- in a manufacturing environment – scheduling of customer and component orders, warehousing and equipment operation, such as set-up times;
- human resources – recruitment and personnel management.

Technical

There is rarely a need to understand the technicalities of a process, although they may be very interesting. The exceptions are when they relate to interdependencies with other areas of the organization or on suppliers.

However, it may be worth looking at the technical areas since this is where some 'obvious' threats to the operation emerge which are not spotted by those who work in that area, perhaps because they are too close to the detail or relate to interdependencies with other processes. Being told by a technician that something 'is too difficult to explain' or 'it cannot happen' is often an indication of a potential problem. Observations of this nature reported to the appropriate manager will add value to the BIA process, although they should not be allowed to divert attention from the BCM programme.

> A telecom specialist was insistent that telephone continuity was assured through a diverse routing of cables from two exchanges run by different companies. A walk down the access road was required to convince him that the access covers for both company's lines were side by side for several hundred metres – a potential target for a misdirected digger bucket.

Interviewing

Interview technique is perhaps rehearsed rather than learned. Undertaking a short pilot BIA and receiving feedback from understanding colleagues is the best way to improve interview technique. Natural selection has given us two eyes, two ears but only one mouth: a good guide to the ideal proportions of their use in an interview.

It is imperative that time is taken to explain to the interviewee or workshop participants the purpose of the BIA and the implications of the responses they give. It may be worth asking a couple of questions to verify their understanding.

An interview of an hour is usually sufficient to gain the required information on a business activity. Longer may be necessary if it appears that the 'activity' may need to be split into two or more for analysis because each has a different time imperative. In this case it may be better to stop after one hour, write up the interview then come back later, as there is a limit to the amount of information that can be absorbed at one time.

Analysis

Some analysis is mechanical:

*   ensuring that all areas of the organization have been addressed;
*   checking that the total resource requirements of all activities add up roughly to their numbers in the organization.

Some analysis is research:

- How do the findings compare with other organizations in the sector? This information may be available informally through industry or BCM forums.

Some analysis is intuitive:

- Do the results make sense? Are they consistent between similar areas of the business?
- Did the interviewee appear to understand the purpose and implications of the questions asked?

Presentation

Presentation skills can be learned and, combined with thorough preparation, will enable the presenter to make a positive impression at a presentation to top management or to a workshop with colleagues. Clarity and enthusiasm are key characteristics of good BIA presentations.

When should we review or redo a BIA?

The BIA as described is a snapshot of the organization's situation. It will soon be out of date and there may be reluctance from management and staff to undertake the whole process again if it required substantial resources or time to undertake.

The conventional answer to the question of frequency of review is annually or when there is a significant change. It is suggested here that a BIA, as an organization wide project, should never be undertaken again because it is too resource intensive. Instead it is recommended that, after an initial BIA as described above, the organization quickly moves to installing an annual BIA process as a regular part of its management programme, as described in the next section.

There is one circumstance when an urgent review of the BIA should be undertaken outside the normal cycle. This is when a disruption has occurred and service delivery has been seriously affected (even it was recovered within the RTO). As a result, the tolerance of customers to further interruptions may be drastically reduced. An 'emergency BIA' may highlight the need for a temporary improvement in the recovery capability of the organization to protect against a repeat disruption for a while. This is in addition to any attempt to prevent a recurrence of the specific incident.

BIA as a process

While the above BIA project approach is suitable for the organization's first BIA, its scale can become a deterrent to keeping the information up to date. The project approach has the following drawbacks:

- It is costly to undertake and difficult to schedule.
- The information required is held by many individuals spread across the organization so data collection is difficult to coordinate.
- The BIA project is not integrated into normal business processes.

Once a suitable structure is clear from an initial BIA, it is suggested that the Strategic, Tactical and Operational hierarchy can be used to break down the BIA 'project' into small elements within a logical structure which can be integrated into normal business review processes.

This structure may be directly applicable to medium-sized organizations, but may need to be expanded (with more levels) or contracted in large or small organizations – but the process should be similar.

The BIA process

The initiator for the BIA process is the organization's strategy statement which is normally produced annually. This should prompt a review of the organization's strategic objectives against its BCM objectives for service delivery of products and services (P&S) using a Strategic BIA to ensure the two are aligned. Given the high level of the statements and their lack of timescales it is not always easy to relate these strategic objectives directly to services, but it is still worth trying. The results from the Strategic BIA then cascade down through the organization to the tactical, and then the operational level.

The elements of the BIA process

'Strategic BIA' is the term used to describe a top management review that:

- identifies the products and services of the organization;
- decides which should be within the scope of the programme; and
- decides their required delivery timescales in the event of a disruption.

By convention, in standards and guidance, the products and services that are within the stated scope of the programme are called 'key' products and services to save having to qualify them as 'in scope of the BCM programme' each time.

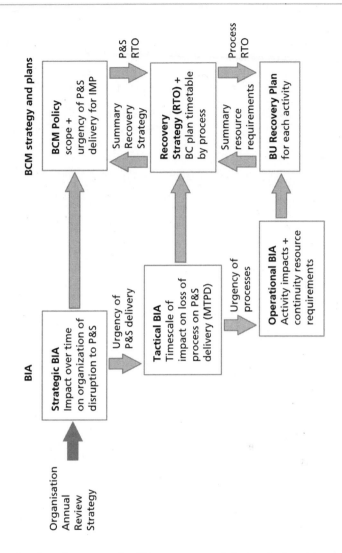

Figure 9   The elements of a BIA process and their relationship to other BCM programme elements

Once the delivery requirements of the key products and services have been fixed, a Tactical BIA can be undertaken to understand the processes that are required to deliver them and how quickly these must be recovered after a disruption to meet the delivery requirements. Once complete, this will be an input into the BC recovery plan.

An Operational BIA is undertaken in each department of the organization and investigates how each activity (of which there may be one or several in each department) operates: the resources that it needs and how it will meet the activity recovery timetable. From this the department's BC recovery plan can be written. The resource requirements from each department can be consolidated to enable appropriate strategies to be selected.

These three elements are described in more detail in Chapters 4, 5 and 6.

4 Strategic BIA

The BCM programme scope should be set out in the organization's BCM policy and therefore already have been completed before the BIA process is initiated. It is considered here because the BIA process can be used to assist top management to set and review the scope in terms of products and services as well as setting the required recovery timescales.

The organization's strategic review

The annual strategic review published by the top management will restate, or revise, the organization's strategic objectives. Given that the BCM programme is expected to relate closely to the objectives of the organization, the publishing of this document should initiate the BIA process as well as prompt a review of the BCM policy.

A change in the strategic objectives of the organization may be reflected in the BCM policy by a change in the scope of the programme, by adding or removing certain products and services, or a change in their priorities, which will affect the scope of the BIA.

Using a BIA to set the scope of the BCM programme

The scope of the BCM programme is defined by the key products and services identified in the BCM policy.

Looking at each product and service in a Strategic BIA, top management may consider that:

- the impacts of non-delivery may not become serious for months, or not at all;
- the organization would still be viable without them;
- the reputation damage that results from the disruption is manageable;
- there are alternative providers to whom the contract or delivery responsibility could be easily passed;
- BCM solutions will be too expensive or not practical.

In these cases they may be excluded from the scope of the BCM programme.

The use of the BIA method, instead of a risk-based approach, ensures that intangible impacts such as reputation are considered, and that the timescale available for making decisions after disruption is identified.

Preparing for the Strategic BIA

Although top management need to make the decisions about scope and delivery timescales, it is necessary to prepare information carefully beforehand that will enable them to understand the nature of the required decisions and to record them in a form that provides a workable structure for the BCM programme.

Understanding the context of the organization

The following information may be useful in understanding the context within which decisions will be made by the top management:

- company/group financial structure: showing the ownership of and external influence on the company and possible availability of external resources in a recovery situation;
- company future strategy: any decisions likely to be taken in the next two/three years that may significantly impact upon the building of a recovery strategy, such as product diversification, expansion, relocation – this may need to be treated in confidence;
- wish list: if the company were to start from scratch, what would be done differently?

Grouping key products and services

The products and services of the organization should be identified and an attempt made to split them logically into a small number of groups. These may be groups of:

- the same type which share roughly the same urgency of delivery;
- customer groups where premium customers are to be treated differently;
- a combination of the above;
- other stakeholder requirements, such as external regulatory reporting.

These groupings may become the basis on which plans are written and a disruption handled, so it is important for them to be meaningful and not too complex.

Estimating a draft MTPD

It will usually be necessary to propose to top management values for the MTPD of each group which they can then challenge to reach a consensus. Therefore research should be conducted to provide appropriate backing for the values proposed. Sources may include:

- previous disruption experience within the organization or similar body;
- company advertising and strategic objectives;
- documented sources, such as contracts, service level agreements (SLAs) and regulations;
- customer surveys, interview data, or marketing opinion;
- the likely impact of a disruption on customers' businesses and their expected response;
- the expected response of competitors;
- financial and other internal impacts on the organization.

Having extracted a set of generic impact types from the above sources, it can be used to populate the table in the next section (Table 1, P&S disruption – Impact by time).

It is also helpful to prepare in advance a draft definition of what constitutes 'intolerable' for each of the selected impact types. Whereas this is relatively easy to define for financial losses, it is more difficult to describe for less tangible loss, such as safety or reputation – but examples may be sufficient.

Possible sources of background information to support these proposals may come from:

- top management – strategic development plans;
- PR/external communications – will provide an understanding of the current capability to mitigate reputational impacts;
- finance – understanding the current cash position, the dynamics of the organization's cash flow and future projections;
- marketing – may be able to provide predictions about customer and competitor behaviour during an incident by analysing the alternatives available, and quantify the loss of market share over time and the cost of winning it back; in the public sector a similar prediction may be available from political analysts;
- insurance – sums insured and terms of any business interruption insurance.

A logistics firm was profitable but had borrowed a huge sum to build an automated sorting facility. Whilst the debt was being paid off, the maintenance of cash flow was an urgent concern as requests for further borrowing would probably be turned down. This had a strong influence on the setting of the MTPDs for delivery services.

Conducting a Strategic BIA

The Strategic BIA requires the input of the top management. Whether this is achieved through a report, workshop or presentation depends on the organization's procedures, but it is important to obtain buy-in to the decisions from a significant proportion of top management – and is an opportunity to make them aware of other aspects of the BCM programme. The views of the project sponsor should be sought as to how this is best achieved.

To ensure consistency of approach it may be worth using a formal time/impact table, one per product and service group (see Table 1).

The factors that emerged as being important during the preparation stage are listed down the side, with space for any additional factors that emerge during the discussion. Those suggested for consideration in the *GPG 2010* are the impact of a disruption on:

* stakeholder or public safety or well-being;
* statutory duties or regulatory requirements;
* reputation;
* financial viability;
* product quality;
* environmental damage;
* other issues specific to the organization.

At present there is no timescale in the column headings. These can be filled in once a pattern emerges from the discussion. The significant points in the timeline were described in Chapter 2 (see section headed Significant time periods in recovery options) as being where alternative strategies became available (a few minutes, days, weeks, months) so, as a minimum, these should be identified as significant. It is also possible that an impact type is not applicable ('n/a') to this product and service group. However, it is probably more important for top managers to come to their own conclusions rather than trying to guide them towards preconceived fixed time slots.

The last column on the table (which may need to be enlarged) should contain an explanation of what factors were taken into account in deciding at what point each impact value would become intolerable. This is vital for subsequent audit and annual review.

PRODUCT OR SERVICE GROUP						
	TIME					
IMPACTS	mins	hrs	days	wks	n/a	Reason
Public/staff safety or welfare						
Media interest/reputation						
Contracts / SLAs						
Financial loss						
Compliance						

Table 1   P&S disruption – Impact by time

Once time periods have been added to the column headings, the table only requires one entry per row: the point in time where the impact becomes intolerable, which could be indicated by a cross.

The points where significant (but tolerable) impact starts to occur could also be indicated. This may help to set the recovery time objective in the strategy stage but it is not necessary. Indeed, the extra detail may confuse by taking the focus off impacts that will cause the organization to fail.

The MTPD can then be set at the point at which the first impact becomes intolerable. The other values (and n/a) prove that other impacts have been considered and discounted.

The above does somewhat contradict what was said earlier – that impacts are cumulative and it is their sum which causes the fatal damage. However, this method seems to provide sufficiently accurate results. If several impacts were estimated to reach the limit at the same time, it may be prudent to decide on an earlier MTPD.

Local authorities in the UK have a statutory duty to provide care for vulnerable people and, under contract, a healthcare company provides home visits to people who need regular medical care. Rotas and nursing staffing are scheduled in advance but these arrangements are frequently upset by nurse unavailability or for a visiting nurse needing to stay longer with a client in difficulty. A control centre plays a pivotal role in managing these frequent changes.

The impacts considered were:

- delays in response causing health deterioration in clients and possibly their death;
- delays causing distress to clients;
- contract breach leading to financial penalties and possible loss of contract;
- loss of future contracts in a highly competitive industry.

A national parliament's administrative body identified three key services:

- plenary meetings of the parliament;
- meetings of the parliamentary committees;
- administrative support for the members of the parliament.

The Strategic BIA considered a range of impacts and agreed recovery timescales. The conclusions were then endorsed by the appropriate parliament committee and made public.

Strategic BIA report

The Strategic BIA report should be a summary of the decisions made by top management giving:

For each product and service (or group) in scope:

- the MTPDs of delivery
- the factors considered in that decision

For each product and service left out of the BCM scope:

- the reasoning behind that decision

Table 1 may provide a suitable reporting format along with explanatory text.

It may be appropriate to include an outline of this information in the organization's policy and for that document to be available to selected or all stakeholders.

5 Tactical BIA

This chapter sets out how to undertake a Tactical BIA which will estimate the MTPD of each process.

Setting the scope

The scope of the Tactical BIA will be determined by which products and services are within the scope of the BIA.

The scope will need to cover:

- each process that directly delivers the product or service (often called 'front-office' or production);
- each process (or part process) that supports the above processes (may be termed the 'back-office');
- suppliers that support any of the above activities.

Figure 10 shows that:

- by excluding Product A, Process A (made up of Activities A1 and A2) are completely out of scope;
- by including Product B within the scope, front-office Process B (made up of Activities B1 and B2) and parts of Processes C and D (and their activities) are within scope. Service D (from a supplier) should also be investigated since Activity B2 is dependent on it;
- if Service C, delivered direct to the customer, was added to the scope it may then be necessary to assure the ability of the outsourcer to deliver to the agreed requirements by assisting them with a BIA.

Initiating a Tactical BIA

The prerequisite of project sponsor agreement has already been noted (see Chapter 3, section headed Sponsorship). For a Tactical BIA the programme sponsor is likely to need to approve or nominate process experts who can be approached for information, although this could also be delegated to departmental heads.

It is usual to initiate contact with these experts with a communication to set the expectations of the meeting.

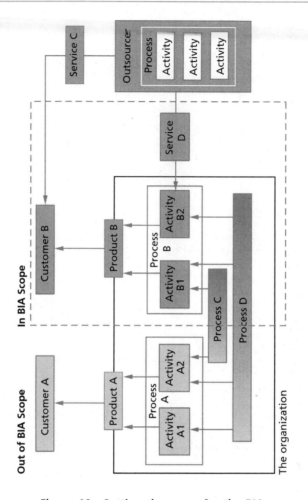

Figure 10   Setting the scope for the BIA

It should cover briefly:

- an explanation that, to develop a BC response, it is necessary to understand the urgency of the various business processes;
- the products and services that are supported by the processes to be discussed;
- prior to the meeting it would be worth considering the impacts that an interruption of the process would have, and whether it is possible to consider this as one or several processes with different requirements;
- a date and time for the meeting and its expected duration.

The note should, of course, make clear the support of the programme sponsor to ensure that the approach is taken seriously.

An alternative approach is to call a short briefing meeting of participants to cover the same ground.

Data collection – choosing the participants

The quality of the data collected will depend heavily on the experience and imagination of the participants in the BIA. The individuals need to know how the activities are performed, though not in detail, and also the dependencies within and outside the organization.

Choosing the correct level of participants is much the same problem as identifying the appropriate level of detail for the BIA: a broad understanding of the business process is required, but apparently small details within an activity can become important. Senior managers should have the wide perspective but are unlikely to have the operational knowledge required (or if they do, it is often out of date).

Process experts are likely to be middle managers in the organization, though they may defer to the expertise of subordinate staff for certain operational details. It is an acquired skill to be able to sift the wealth of data for the appropriate level of generality and crucial detail.

Data collection – the data

The Tactical BIA determines the timescale of resumption of each activity that enables the targets for continuity of product and service delivery to be achieved. The appropriate measure for this (which is a requirement in BS 25999-2) is the MTPD.

To capture the MTPD alone would make it difficult to justify its value so the nature and timescale of each of the impacts (where relevant) should be plotted in a table. The impact which most quickly hits the tolerable limit will determine the choice, but it is important for later audit and review that it can be shown that other impacts have been considered.

Table 2 comes from the table completed for the Strategic BIA (Table 1) – and a similar table will be required for each process.

PROCESS							
RELATED PRODUCTS/SERVICES							
	TIME						
IMPACTS	1 hr	8 hrs	1 day	1 wk	2 wks	2 mths	Reason
Public/staff safety or welfare							
Media interest/reputation							
Contracts/SLAs							
Financial loss							
Compliance							
Supplier confidence							
Backlog							

Table 2   Process disruption – Impact by time

Note that a couple of 'internal' impacts have now been added to the table that originated in the Strategic BIA. These may be felt by some of the process experts to be particularly relevant to the rate at which impacts on external stakeholders might increase. However, the overall number should be limited to about eight impacts; otherwise discussion takes too long.

Times have also been added as a result of the Strategic BIA findings. The timings in the example are for illustration only – they will depend on the urgency of the business. For example, if the Strategic BIA found that no products and services need be delivered for a week, it is unlikely that there would be any activity requiring resumption much more quickly than that, unless the activity takes a significant time to complete, such as in manufacturing. Here it needs to be made clear whether the MTPD refers to the point of starting or of completing the process. An understanding of the process and, perhaps, a more complex form may be required in this case.

If the RTOs of the relevant products and services have already been set, this step could also be used to determine an RTO for the process.

Data collection – methods

There are various ways of collecting the required data, which include:

- interviews
- questionnaires
- workshops
- quick BIAs

The choice of method may be dictated by the time available, locations to be covered or experience. Each method has its strengths and weaknesses, which are analysed and summarized below.

Interviews

Face-to-face or telephone interviews are the most time-consuming ways to collect the required data, but they are likely to yield more meaningful results because:

- answers can be challenged immediately;
- an interview generates more buy-in and therefore, perhaps, more responsible answers, and may generate an interest which can be harnessed in subsequent phases of the programme;
- issues can be explored beyond the initial scope of the interview that may enhance understanding of the business.

Interviews must be minuted and it is recommended that a standard form be used to ensure consistency and completeness of coverage. An example of such a form, assembled from the guidance in this chapter, is in the Appendix. The form, or a narrative extract, can then be sent to the respondent to agree its contents. It is important to give the respondent a deadline after which agreement will be assumed if no comment is received.

Questionnaire

Questionnaires are easy to distribute to large numbers of staff and are useful if the respondents are widespread and software is available to manage and collate the results.

It is possible to create a questionnaire from a form similar to that used for interviews. However, the need to explain the context of the questions may require a text which is so long that respondents will not read it. The responses, therefore, may be difficult to interpret because the questions have not been understood; nor is there an opportunity for any immediate challenge to them.

For this reason it is unlikely that questionnaires will provide a reliable technique for an organization's first BIA. However, once the process of BIA is embedded, respondents have received training and results from the last BIA are available for review, questionnaires can then provide an effective means of maintaining the information. Nonetheless, any significant changes or anomalies should be followed up with interviews.

Software packages for conducting BIAs are available, most of which are integrated into BC planning products. The comments above should be considered when planning to use these tools. It is unlikely that the templates provided will fit the needs of the organization without some modification.

Workshop

Getting process experts together can be a quick and very effective way to collect and verify process information. The perceived urgency of processes can be challenged by those in the group, which should make the results realistic and consensual. Sometimes arguments will persist and it helps for the workshop leader to be seen to be independent and have a good background knowledge of the organization.

The workshop can follow a similar outline as that described for interviews, but the process experts can outline their conclusions and have this subjected to scrutiny by the others. Interrelationships can be mapped for those parts of the organization represented and the most urgent highlighted.

It may be useful to select an incident scenario and use the situation that develops to discuss the impacts that would arise. This requires careful facilitating since the discussion will tend to focus on attempts at operational recovery rather than on the impacts of the failure of each process on the organization.

Alternatively, two workshops could be scheduled: the first to give a briefing on how to fill in a questionnaire to be completed and sent in; the second, a few weeks later, to display the collated information and discuss discrepancies.

Mixture of methods

In practice, the choice of methods may be a hybrid of those mentioned above and will depend on how such things are normally done within the organization.

A briefing meeting may save some time on explanation during an interview and allow process experts to consider their responses in advance.

Questionnaire response quality may be better if it is known that an interview will follow; or the responses can be used to select a sample for interview.

A final briefing of process experts will be a useful endorsement for findings and provide the opportunity to explain the next steps in the BCM programme.

SWOT analysis of data collection methods

Table 3 sets out some of the strengths, weaknesses, opportunities and tips (SWOT) of the various approaches to BIA data collection.

Interview

Strengths	Weaknesses
• Involves staff and raises awareness • Interviewer gains knowledge of people and functions • Discovers actual impacts (near misses) • Addresses personal views and fears	• Time consuming • Need to prepare • May use more staff time • Questionnaire draft still needed • Personal response • Lacks consistency if more than one interviewer

Opportunities	Tips
• Use for senior participants • Use where subjective assessment is required • Use where awareness is a requirement	• Formalize interview structure • Interview in location • Try to interview in context of business deliverables not departmental aims • Take time to explain purpose of BIA

Table 3a   SWOT analysis of BIA data collection methods

Questionnaire

Strengths	Weaknesses
• Easy to analyse • Easier to standardize response • 'Hard-copy' evidence • Can be automated • Software available for remote entry	• Questionnaire fatigue • Interpretation of questions by respondent • Possibility of error in questions nullifying the results • Lack of involvement • Miss soft issues • Miss major issues through not challenging response
Opportunities	**Tips**
• In a mature BCM organization • When data can be numerical or ranked • As a follow-up • If the number of respondents is high • Remote locations	• Database or spreadsheets for graphs • Keep data requirements tight • Verify data • Mix with interviews

Table 3b   SWOT analysis of BIA data collection methods

Workshop

Strengths	Weaknesses
• Cross-department perspective • Brain storming • Shows organization's commitment • Fewer distractions • More professional	• Difficult to timetable • Difficult to deal with dissent and internal politics in a group • Facilitation skills required • Lots of preparation
Opportunities	**Tips**
• When rapid results required • High level of organizational commitment	• Sell to management on the basis of cost savings • Prepare it well – you only get one chance!

Table 3c   SWOT analysis of BIA data collection methods

Conducting an interview

Interview with manager or process expert

The interview should open with a discussion about the one or more processes to be discussed. This should concentrate on the inputs and outputs of the process rather than the detail of its operation and constituent activities.

The definition of a process (a set of activities with roughly the same MTPD) should be remembered during this discussion. It is possible that the respondent's area of responsibility may cover a number of activities undertaking a similar operation but with different urgency. In a call centre, for example, there may be different types of call being received – and some may require a more urgent response than others. It is then a consideration whether, for the BIA analysis, this process should be split into two or more processes with a different MTPD for each, or whether this can be better described as a number of activities within a single process.

The purpose of BCM may need to be briefly explained to the respondents before the impacts of disruption are discussed, in order to help them understand how their answers will be used. In particular, it needs to be stressed that the interest is in the impact of the disruption, not its possible cause.

It may be difficult for a respondent to visualize how one process or activity alone can be disrupted with the rest of the organization still functioning but, as usual, the real world provides instances of this. On the day after the department barbecue or the office night out staff may be laid low for several days by food poisoning. A couple of manufacturing companies have recently suffered a rapid and permanent loss of production staff following lottery syndicates winning the jackpot. Alien abduction of their team is another explanation that may raise a smile – and is reputedly a concern in certain parts of the world.

For the front-line activities the impacts and timescales will be relatively easy to relate to the organization's products and services. If several serial or concurrent processes are involved in delivering the product or service then these interviews need to explore these interrelationships and their time parameters. Interviews in the back office should focus more on the internal relationships and the speed with which their inactivity would cause issues in other departments.

Assessing the impact of a disruption to the process should utilize the same set of impact types that were developed for the Strategic BIA. Additional internal impacts, such as loss of supplier confidence, product quality and backlog management, should also be considered.

The most common difficulty experienced during interviews with process experts is that they find it difficult to visualize the disruption of their activity unless it has actually happened recently. Their initial guess at an 'MTPD' is often four hours – which is really the limit of their imagination.

If this initial response seems unlikely, challenges can be made such as:

- Would you call staff back at 5.00 pm if you were evacuated at 1.00 pm?
- Has there been a recent interruption to service? If so, for how long?
- What happens during holiday and festival periods that last for more than a week – does work continue or can it be delayed?

Reaching a best estimate for the MTPD is the function of the impact/time table since this challenges the respondent to identify the actual impacts that would occur if the process was disrupted. The timescale at which each impact reaches its tolerable limit should be indicated on the impact/time table. If the view of the activity specialist does not tally with that of the Strategic BIA the reasons for this should be explored, since it is possible that some factor is visible at this level but has been overlooked by top management. Such factors may include legal or contractual obligations or operational constraints.

The MTPD can be stated in a number of ways depending on its time-relationship with the MTPD of the product delivery. For example, if a product needs to be delivered to a customer within 48 hours and the delivery process (picking, checking, loading and journey time activities) is 8 hours then its MTPD could be described as 40 hours after the disruption or 8 hours before the delivery. The later method is probably easier to understand but may be more difficult to tabulate alongside other processes.

The timescales of the reliance on internal and external suppliers should be discussed and listed (with the exception of utilities and common supplies). The timescale of dependence on other departments should also be understood. For external suppliers copies of contracts or service level agreement should be sought – at least for supplies delivery of which is 'just-in-time' or where the on-site inventory would quickly be exhausted.

A common difficulty that arises in these discussions is the tendency of the process expert to try to identify operational solutions and mitigation measures rather than concentrate on the impacts and timescale of the disruption. These measures could be noted for consideration in the BCM strategy stage but should not distract from the main purpose of the interview.

Overall, a BIA interview of a process expert should take about an hour unless unexpected issues arise.

Background documents search

The following documents may be relevant to the Tactical BIA and to assess current recovery capability:

- the company personnel structure, giving management/departmental structure and names and titles of managers;
- regulations or statutory duties applicable to this sector;
- insurance policies – especially business interruption insurance (the wording of which must be read to check the cover and exclusions under various scenarios);
- availability of recovery facilities – including contracted recovery sites, other locations or formal or informal agreements with partners;
- a previous BIA;
- reports and anecdotes on past incidents experienced by the organization, those in the same sector or neighbourhood.

Analyse and verify data

Once the Tactical BIA data has been collected, or even while it is coming in, the results need to be collated, verified and analysed.

Various mechanical checks can be performed:

- Have all activities been identified? A full organization chart will usually answer this.
- Have the interrelationships been identified by both source and destination activities? A diagram such as that in Figure 11 may help to check for completeness.

With the activities arranged in urgency order:

- Does the order make sense?
- Is the order consistent with existing strategies and previous BIA results? (If not, perhaps the previous BIA and existing strategy were incorrect.)
- Is it consistent with reports or anecdotes of the response to past incidents?
- Will the results require expensive recovery strategies? Should they be double-checked for correctness?
- Does the BCM Steering Committee (or similar body) agree with the findings, or is there a need for a management workshop to discuss the results further?
- What are other companies in the same sector doing? This information may be available from consultants, attendance at BCM forums or informal contact with BCM personnel in other similar organizations.

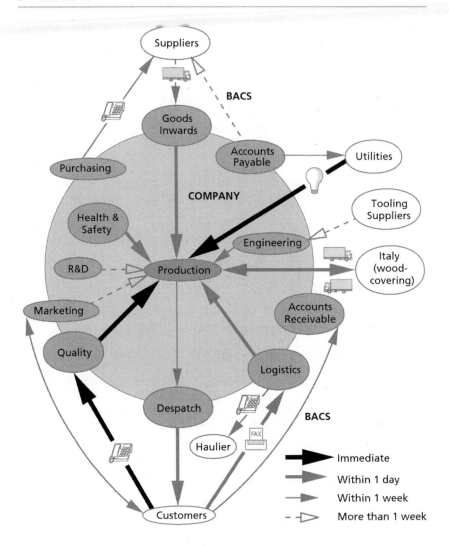

Figure 11   Example interrelationship diagram showing urgency of interactions

Consider also:

- The knowledge of the interviewees: can any questionable or contradictory details be verified?
- Has the BIA has adopted the appropriate level of detail? Are there too many processes or activities to be manageable or too few to be meaningful when it comes to writing recovery plans?
- Is there a consensus about the results? This can be checked by sending out report segments to contributors.

Completing the process

Reporting the findings

The findings of the Tactical BIA are likely to be delivered in two forms to management:

- a report
- a presentation

Tactical BIA report

The Tactical BIA will be a more detailed document than the Strategic BIA since it will look at each process (or activity), not just the products and services. Its purpose is to identify the urgency of each process that is required to deliver those products and services within the BIA scope.

There is no standard format for a BIA report, so what follows is a format that has evolved over a number of years but is adapted to the needs of each business – not copied and pasted. Organizations may have their own formats or layouts which should be followed instead provided they cover the same content.

A typical format for a Tactical BIA will consist of the following sections:

- Executive summary
- Organization background
- Project background
- Current recovery capability
- Impact of loss of each process
- Summary of business impact
- Appendices

The possible content of each of these sections will be considered below.

The BIA report may be supplemented by an outline recovery strategy which describes in general terms the options available that would satisfy the recovery requirements identified. This will allow the top management to make initial decisions on the future direction and funding of the BCM programme based on the findings of the BIA. The content of this strategy report is out of the scope of this text.

BIA executive summary

The BIA summary should be concise – one or two pages at most. The headings could be:

- Objective of the BIA: setting out what the BIA will demonstrate;
- Current recovery capability: how well the organization can currently meet its delivery obligations;
- Gap analysis and resulting impacts: where it falls short and what would be the consequences (which should already have been identified in the Strategic BIA);
- Conclusion: what needs to be done about it.

Organization background

It may seem odd to write a section on the organization for those who should know this already, but this section sets the context of the BIA at the time it was written and can therefore be used at the next revision to identify subsequent changes. It is surprising how quickly people forget what happened and at what time in an organization's history. This section may protect the author against accusations of ignoring information which was not available at the time.

Possible headings include:

- Structure and ownership of the organization: if part of a group, this may include the extent to which the group members and owners have been involved in this analysis;
- Stakeholders: identification of the main stakeholders;
- Location(s): the geographic extent of the organization (the scope of the report is detailed in the next section);
- Products and services: a list of all P&S in the organization (the scope of the report is detailed in the next section);
- Future developments?: What information was available about future developments within the organization such as mergers, location closures etc.? Information that is withheld may have led to different conclusions if it had been available.

> On future developments: A company repairing consumer
> electrical equipment was under contract to several major
> retailers. It operated out of two sites which were separated by
> 15 kms but the second site could not act as a back-up for the
> main site because of a lease issue. Having listened to an
> attempt to present a viable recovery strategy, the CEO
> interrupted the presentation with 'Didn't I tell you we bought
> another (third) site last month?'

Project background

Though the BCM practitioner is, of course, clear on what a BIA is, it will
need to be explained to the reader of the report. It is not unusual for
top management to assume the Tactical BIA is the completed BC plan –
though, to be fair, some BC plans look like BIAs, with much on what
might happen but little practical recovery instruction.

This section should set out the expectations of the report that follows,
and these headings may help to structure this section:

- The need for a BCM response: a brief explanation of the situations in
  which a BC response might be required. This could highlight recent
  incidents.
- Objectives of the BCM programme: what the BCM programme should
  achieve – an effective response to those situations above.
- Purpose of this report: how a BIA ensures that the response is
  appropriate and what happens next.
- Concepts: an explanation of MTPD and how it is estimated for
  products, services and activities.
- Project scope: which products and services are analysed in this report;
  which locations/regions are analysed, and whether this was a
  complete survey or locations were sampled.
- Project methods: how the BIA was conducted – a copy of the survey
  form may be an appropriate attachment.

An example of scope from a report:

> This report considers the impact of serious physical incidents – which could threaten
> business survival – occurring at the site. The impact will spread to other locations and
> these are identified. Incidents at other company sites are excluded from this project.
> It examines incidents outside the core competence of the business, so commercial
> issues such as marketing failures, lack of profitability and product quality are not
> covered in this report. The impact of the group's long-term strategy for the business
> has also not been examined.
> This report, and the outline recovery strategy developed from it, have taken into

account the building of the new computer suite but have not examined the business processes to be undertaken within the new office building, since this information was not available.

Current recovery capability

The organization's current capability to manage disruptions should be critically analysed to show whether it is sufficient or would be ineffective. For example, the speed with which current recovery capabilities can be made operational can be compared to the timescale required to recover the process.

Aspects to consider in this section may include:

- insurance – a summary of covers, exclusions and limitations, particularly for business interruption insurance;
- other company facilities – an examination of any assumptions about the use of other locations or resources for recovery;
- any stakeholder assistance – an evaluation of assumptions made about help to be expected from associated organizations such as partners, customers or local authorities;
- Contracted recovery and maintenance services – this may include workspace or IT DR contracts;
- Any recent incidents – this may help to evaluate the effectiveness of the measures above, and also convince the reader that disruptions do happen.

Impact of loss of each process

This will form the largest section of the report. It outlines the impact of disruption of each process on the overall operation of the organization.

The section should start with a statement of the agreed strategic level delivery timescales from which these process requirements will mostly derive. The order in which each of the processes is described should follow a logical sequence which will depend on the nature of the business. For example, the order of a commercial company could be: marketing, sales, production, accounts, support services. Alternatively each process could be grouped by department/division or by product or service.

Each process should be considered using the following headings, where applicable:

- a brief description of the process;
- the products and services that rely on this process;
- interdependencies with other activities – internal and external;

- direct and indirect impacts on service delivery;
- impacts of disruption to this process, over time – which may be quantified and qualified. These may be:
  - external – causing disruption to product and service delivery;
  - internal – causing impacts within the organization that might indirectly disrupt delivery: for example, an inability to pay suppliers may stop the flow of materials;
- maximum tolerable period of disruption – an estimate based on the external and internal impacts noted above.

An example of a process described in a report:

Department: Technical Support

Technical Support provides advice to all business areas on Life and Pensions. In particular, it checks all literature such as adverts before appointed representatives (ARs) are allowed to publish them.

It manages campaigns from inception to market. Peak times for pension processing are launches in January to meet peak season in February and March. Failure of launch in January could potentially lose most of the annual new sales.

ARs (although not tied) generally offer new clients products from only two or three insurance companies because this minimizes their paperwork and background study.

Priority activities

- literature check for ARs providing a 2-day turnaround;
- pensions helpline – immediate response expected;
- pensions transfer business is usually expected within 5 days;
- technical queries from Customer Services may be urgent.

Costs of loss

Immediately: There would be dissatisfaction, and possibly compensation requests, from ARs if they cannot get approval for literature, since they could lose earnings.

Within one week: It is expected that a significant number of ARs would threaten action to recover lost commission, choose to place new business with another company and transfer their loyalties elsewhere as soon as possible. ARs often work together and would probably suggest to colleagues that they do the same.

Conclusion

- Maximum tolerable period of disruption – 1 week
- Reason: loss of new business, loss of ARs and reputation in market

Summary of impacts

In this final section the process detail can be synthesized to describe a timeline of how impacts would develop after a disruption.

The disruption should be non-specific, perhaps an indefinite denial of access to a site or absence of staff. One or more disruption types or extent (single or multi-site) may be described but the 'story' should be kept simple. A narrative style is appropriate since the objective is to persuade the reader to take action as a result of the credibility of the accumulating impacts rather than the scenario.

It may be useful to display some of the summary information in the form of diagrams:

- relationships between activities, products and service (see Figure 11).
- MTPD by process – in order of urgency (see Figure 12).

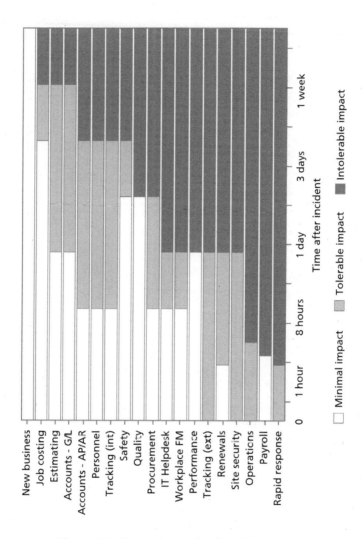

Figure 12   Example graph of activity MTPDs

An example of a summary of impacts (from the same report as previous example):

Timetable of an incident

The following analysis shows the cumulative impact of loss of business processes.

On the first day of a loss of access to site, these would be highly visible but not business-threatening:

- Unit prices missing from next morning's press
- Call centre not operational

On day two the above processes would continue to be missed. The continued absence of the call centre would become business-threatening since the backlog of calls will already exceed the 'spare' capacity between 8.30 am and 5.30 pm.

On day three the impact of additional processes is added to those above.

- Non-standard illustrations cannot be supplied to ARs and IFAs.
- New business is lost since the delays in acceptance result in cancellation.
- Pensions benefits quotations cannot be given.
- Uncollected premiums exceed €10M.

By the end of a week further issues will create additional pressures, in particular:

- Commission payments to ARs will have stopped.
- ARs attempt to recover lost earnings.
- Delays to cheque issue to claimants would have high-profile media attention.

Delivering the report format

Whilst experience of report writing is obviously a necessary skill, a few points that follow may assist the acceptance of the report:

- The use of maps and diagrams, and even photographs if relevant, helps to make the document easier to read by varying the page layout and caters for those who prefer graphics to text.
- Real incidents can be interpolated at appropriate points in the text in the style of a newspaper cutting (as in this text) to counter the 'it won't happen here' incident sceptics.
- The circulation of the document should be confirmed with the project sponsor since some of the information contained in the report may be confidential, such as planned future developments.
- The agreement of all contributors should be sought. This need not be done for the whole document: contributors need only see the relevant parts. Similarly the endorsement of the sponsor and top managers should be sought before the report is finalized.

> A presentation to top management is not the place to discover that there is fundamental disagreement with your report. This may not be a doubt over the findings or opinions but could be a blocking tactic by an 'under-pressure' individual to delay progress, or result from some internal power struggle within the management. It could also be a scepticism of the need for BCM, so come prepared with examples of real-life topical incidents and examples of positive outcomes. Being told that nuclear warheads were regularly driven past their front (and only) entrance got the attention of one Board.

Presenting the Tactical BIA to top management

Top management may request that the findings of the BIA are presented to them as there are likely to be significant financial implications of a recovery strategy in a newly started BCM programme. This can be a daunting prospect if you are not accustomed to meeting with top management and, as always, preparation is the key to success.

It is likely that the Strategic BIA discussions took place several months ago and that top management have not had time to read your full Tactical BIA report. You should circulate a paper to them beforehand reminding them of earlier decisions, summarize the current report and outline the strategy options, pointing out the decisions that need to be made by them.

The problem with presenting a BIA on its own is that it is 'bad news'. One approach to the presentation is to describe the proposed BCM recovery strategy, and refer to the BIA report only if there is a question as to why a particular strategy is appropriate.

Whilst it is not possible to quantitatively demonstrate the benefits of a particular strategy (because this requires assumptions on the frequency of disruptions that cannot be backed up by evidence), the potential costs of doing nothing (from the BIA) should be pointed out.

One aspect to stress is the strategic implications of the proposed BCM strategy. Some impacts may be mitigated by future decentralization or diversification – and this should be pointed out.

A presentation of a BIA was being given by a consultant to the directors of an insurance firm which operated from two locations. The consultant had not been told that they were planning to move to one larger building the following year. However, they announced at the meeting that they had decided to abandon the move because, having read and understood the BIA report, they realized the increased resilience that two sites gave to the company.

Some BCM strategies may have benefits for day-to-day business activities and so may justify expenditure on this wider criteria.

The same insurance firm struggled with computer response at the start of each month as end of month reporting slowed the system to a crawl. As part of the BCM strategy, a back-up computer system was installed in their second building with data being copied overnight via a network connection. The end of month reporting could then be run off the back-up machine, so the primary machine's response time was not affected.

Remember to leave plenty of time for questions and discussion during, and at the end of, the presentation.

6 Operational BIA

The Strategic and Tactical BIAs have set the MTPDs of the products and services and their associated activities. In the Operational BIA we identify the urgency and resource needs of each activity within each department that together make up the processes of the organization.

In a small and simple organization it is possible that the analysis of processes will have provided sufficient detail to enable recovery strategies to be determined, in which case the identification of individual activities will not be required and the step can be limited to determining the resource requirements of each activity. In a large organization, a more detailed activity-level understanding is required of the operation to enable departmental recovery requirements to be documented and recovery plans to be written.

In a large department it is probable that the head of department is able to determine the urgency of the processes in the Tactical BIA but requires those who actually undertake the work, or who supervise them, to identify the staffing, applications and other resources required for each activity within it. In a smaller department it is more likely that the head of department will be able to answer on both counts.

Even for an initial BIA it is worthwhile to request the appointment of a BC Coordinator for the department who can undertake this detailed research. Once the BIA process becomes embedded that person will take on the full responsibility of developing and maintaining the departmental plan. This individual therefore needs to have or be able to acquire knowledge of the processes.

An initial BIA will make the first attempt to identify the appropriate division of the department's processes into activities. Subsequent BIAs should always review the scope of each activity since this is where most operational changes will be reflected.

Activity urgency

The urgency of an activity will be set by the urgency of the process of which it is a constituent part. If the sequence of activities required to perform the process is complex, or if an activity takes a significant length of time to achieve, this should be noted and may need to be taken into account in setting the overall recovery timescales of the process.

It is not strictly necessary to assess the impact of failure of the activity since assessment of the failure of the process of which it is part will have been carried out at the tactical level. Indeed, it is often difficult for those managing at an operational level to understand the full implications of a disruption. Nonetheless it provides a useful cross-check and may identify some unexpected impacts, particularly those related to dependencies on other departments and suppliers. It also provides a useful discussion at a BCM training event to operational staff providing or collecting the information.

Quantifying resource requirements

To understand the continuity resource requirements, the resource needs of each activity should be quantified and aggregated at various levels for use in the BCM strategy. The quantification of resources should focus on those that might need to be made available in advance; details that can be addressed internally by the department itself should be addressed when developing departmental recovery plans.

It may appear that an activity's resource requirement is going to best be described as a phased recovery over time, rather than a return to normal at a specific time. This may be the case when an activity is supporting services with a range of MTPDs. This is often the case for back-office activities which may provide support to all the organization's service delivery.

This can be managed in various ways:

• Phasing the resource requirements within a single process
• Splitting the process into two or more phased activities
• Splitting the process into several activities

Process:	ACCOUNTS		
Time:	Day 1	Day 3	Day 10
Staff nos.	1	5	15

Table 4a   Phased resource requirements

Activity:	ACCOUNTS (supervisor)		
MTPD:	Day 1	Day 3	Day 10
Staff nos.	1	1	1

Activity:	ACCOUNTS (invoicing)		
MTPD:	Day 1	Day 3	Day 10
Staff nos.	0	2	4

Activity:	ACCOUNTS (payments)		
MTPD:	Day 1	Day 3	Day 10
Staff nos.	0	2	10

Table 4b   Splitting into several phased activities

Activity No.	Process:	ACCOUNTS		
	Activity MTPD:	Day 1	Day 3	Day 10
1	Supervisor	1	1	1
2	Priority Invoicing		1	1
3	Other invoicing			2
4	Priority payments		1	1
5	Other payments			8
6	Payments backlog		2	2
	Total staff	1	5	15

Table 4c   Splitting the process into several activities with fixed resource

Tables 4a to 4c illustrate three possible ways of describing the resource requirements of an Accounts activity and show, essentially, the same resource requirements information. Staff numbers only are shown here for simplicity, but the full resource requirements should be tabulated.

Estimating the required build-up of staff over a period of time, without identifying the component activities, is not easy and may be difficult to verify and maintain. Also to expect staff to undertake only part of an activity after a disruption without clear prioritization may overwhelm them.

Splitting the process into two or more separate activities with separate MTPDs but phased resources is an option but it may complicate maintenance and recovery planning.

It is therefore suggested that this issue is addressed at the activity level – as in Table 4c. Here, phased process resumption is described as the initiation of a sequence of activities each with an MTPD and fixed resources that together give a timely and effective recovery. The activity resource detail is held within the departmental plan, the process resource summary at a higher level. This option keeps the recording of resource requirements simple, although it does add to the number of separate activities to record and maintain.

The decision on which method to adopt should be heavily influenced by it being practical for those who may have to manage a recovery and be understandable to those running the business.

The MTPD timescales will be replaced by RTOs once during the BCM strategy phase.

Staff

Most activities have a staffing requirement. This could be roughly estimated as a proportion of a department's numbers, but it is most useful if numbers of staff are assigned to particular activities. Some staff may undertake a number of activities over a period but their time can be allocated pro rata. However, it is not necessary to do this with precision and, in practice, whole numbers are usually sufficient. Where the workforce varies periodically, the maximum figure should be recorded.

The information required for recovery capacity planning does not, at this stage, require an understanding of the complexity of part-time or job sharing. Therefore 'full-time equivalent' numbers should be used for consistency.

Where it is clear that a significant effort will be required to clear backlogs rapidly after an incident, it may be appropriate to estimate the staff numbers required and the likely duration of the backlog clearance. This could be added to the analysis as a separate, temporary, activity to ensure that it is included in department plans.

To assist recovery planning the staff resource requirement should make note of specialist skills or qualifications required for an activity. 'Key' individuals may also be identified that are pivotal to an activity; this should prompt an assessment of how the knowledge or skills of these individuals can be shared or documented in case they are unavailable during an incident.

Location

Although alternative workspace requirements are often defined by their desk capacity, some activities are dependent on their location, or the size, facilities or layout of the available space. For example, close proximity to customers may be important.

ICT systems

The identification of the information and communications technologies (ICT) requirements of each activity is vital to enable the appropriate IT disaster recovery strategies to be developed. The capacity, configuration and recovery timetable of alternative ICT services will depend on this information.

Identifying the required ICT services and translating them into ICT requirements is rarely an easy task because:

- ICT application names often differ from the names by which users know them.
- A single user application may access a number of ICT applications – and may pass data to and from other applications in overnight processes.
- ICT back-up and restoration is usually done by machine or disk, which may contain data from a number of different applications with different restoration priorities.

One can reduce the complexity of the application information collected by assuming that the organization's standard desktop configuration will be available and therefore recording only the requirements for specialized applications for each activity.

Other equipment

The requirements for other equipment – such as printers, dongles and copiers – should be noted, particularly for the more urgent activities or where the equipment is specialist and may have a long lead time to acquire.

In a manufacturing environment this area can become very complex and decisions may need to be made about the level of detail to which BCM strategy and planning will be taken. If relocation of production is the appropriate strategy, it will probably be the responsibility of the production team, not the BCM, to ensure that equipment and products are compatible across sites.

Information

Activities usually depend on the availability of information. This may be electronic data from computer systems, paperwork or reference documents. There are two key issues to be considered at this point: currency and accessibility.

The currency of the data needs to be determined in advance to define the back-up strategy of ICT data and paper information. If computer systems need to be restored from back-up media, the data may be so out of date that the activity cannot operate effectively. Recreating the lost data may be impossible, or take so much time that the MTPD is exceeded. It is therefore possible to estimate a 'maximum tolerable data loss' – that is, the minimum currency of data beyond which it is so out of date that recovery is impossible. This applies also to paper records, their scanning and storage.

Timely access to information is also important if the activity depends on its availability. This may include reference books, drawings, expense claims or written staff records. Some records may be vital, others just useful to have. In the BCM strategy planning stage work needs to go into identifying the means of providing this information within the required timescales.

Suppliers

The reliance on suppliers and contractors should be documented for each activity. At the tactical level time dependence on suppliers was noted. At the operational level details of the goods and services supplied and the contractual commitments for the more urgent activities should be sought and, perhaps later, the contract manager should be asked to check on their BCM capability. For the less urgent activities, or where there are adequate alternatives, there is less requirement for detail.

Only supplies specific to a few activities should be dealt with at this level. Common utilities such as power and heating will be addressed at the corporate level in the BCM strategy.

Work in progress

The issue of work in progress should also be addressed with each specific activity. This may involve looking at the detail of the process so that potential data losses can be identified where information exists only in one place, such as:

- documents received from external sources (such as orders) which have not yet been processed;
- paper copies (such as notes or drawings) that have not been copied or entered onto computer systems;
- phone calls which have not been processed or logged;
- computer data which has been entered but has not yet been backed up off-site.

The potential impact of the loss of each data item should be evaluated; this should take into account:

- the cost of the loss or reinstatement;
- the ease and speed of recreating the data from other sources.

Although loss of an individual item of data may be trivial, the cumulative impact of many items may be significant.

This level of detail may not be feasible in an initial BIA but should be attempted in a later review since the ability to recover may be threatened by the loss of this information.

This data should be useful input into any information management strategy being implemented within an organization.

Workarounds

There may be alternative ways in which the activity could be operated without certain resources. This could include:

- working manually during a computer failure;
- not doing part of the activity;
- utilizing resources from another location or organization.

If these are subject to any time limits or have significant impacts on other areas they should be noted. They may require additional information or facilities to be available pre-incident, which may require procedural changes.

Backlogs

The means by which backlogs could be managed and cleared could be discussed. This could include:

- use of staff from other areas of the organization (for which they may require training);
- recruitment of temporary staff (which may be covered by insurance);
- subcontracting.

Threat minimization

Although specific threats do not feature in the BIA, an interview that aims to understand the processes and activities may throw up some obvious operational threats that may, or may not, have been identified by the process owner. This will add value to the findings but these details must not distract from developing the BCM strategy.

Process improvement for resilience

In going through the activities (or when looking at interrelationships), improvements to the process which may improve efficiency or resilience may become obvious. These should be documented and passed to the responsible person.

Collection of operational data

Resource requirements

In collecting the resource requirements, it has been assumed that the comments made in the earlier chapters on resources and backlogs have been noted. Therefore, we need to document the current staffing and other resources (and any extras) that will be required to be operational before the activity's MTPD.

Much of the resource information is of a straightforward quantitative nature and can be collected by questionnaire. Collection of the additional information is better carried out, at least initially, by an interview giving the chance to challenge assumptions and explore alternative solutions.

The following text illustrates an example of a form for collecting the resource and additional information. It also aims to inform and confirm the urgency of each activity within the department (the first line of the form was already filled in). It was preceded by a short training session and followed up by an interview in some cases. For illustration, the explanatory text used on the form has been included below.

> ### BIA - Collection of resource information
>
> Objective: What we are trying to understand from this exercise is the resource requirements of the various activities within each office as well as to confirm with you the urgency of the various things you do. Therefore consider, if (for example) office space was short, what activities have to be done now, what can be left until tomorrow, the day after or later still (though still need to be done some time!)? It should help you to consider what would happen if you did not complete that activity: what impact would it have, and on whom?
>
> The urgency of some activities may depend on what else is going on in the business (for example, seasonal variations) and you are asked to indicate this.
>
> Do ask for assistance or further explanation perhaps after you have made a start to ensure you are on the right track.

Term	Explanation
Process	This is the high-level process of which this activity is part, and determines the urgency of the work you are doing.
Activity	To work to the required level of detail for this exercise, an activity is something done by one or more staff.
Impact of disruption	What would happen if this activity stopped: who would it affect? There may be several impacts.
Urgency	How quickly would these impacts become serious? Does this depend on the time of the month (M) or is the requirement continuous (C)?
Inputs	What information or other inputs drive the activity from within or outside the office? Where does it come from?
Staff	How many staff are required to fulfil the activity (on average)? If the peak staff requirement is significantly higher please give a separate figure and the peak time.
Systems	What systems are used? Ignore standard software but do identify where external contact by email or internet is a key part of the activity.
Resources	What resources do you need? (e.g. paper records, reference books, physical objects)
External services	What contracted or external services do you depend on directly (ignore common utilities such as electricity).
Other dependencies	Is there anything else the office depends on not already mentioned?
Output/deliverable	What results from this activity? What is its purpose? This may be the final result or may become an input to another office's business process.
Recovery of work in progress	If you lost all work done today, what would be the impact?
Workarounds	Are there any other ways in which work could be done – perhaps manually/externally?
Backlogs	Will backlogs cause problems? How might they be managed or cleared?

Table 5a   Explanation of terms in Activity data form

Operational Business Impact Analysis form (one per activity)						
Dept	Activ-ity Ref	Task name	Type	Urgency RTO (days)	Product/service	Process
SAL	SAL01	*Telephone order processing*	*C*	*2*	*All*	*Order processing*

Dept name	Normal staff	Day 0	Day 1	Day 2	Day 5	Day 10	Day 30	Comment
Sales	*18*	*0*	*0*	*25*	*18*	*18*	*18*	*Order prioritization required on resumption + extra staffing for 2 days*

Dept Group	Dept Head	Dept BCC1	Dept BCC2
S&M	*Mary Dishforth*	*Richard Hawes*	*Joan Calcutt*

MTPD (days)	Impact of loss
5	*No phone orders; financial and reputational impacts*

Inputs	*Telephone orders from customer*
Outputs	*Picking lists to warehouse, shortages to purchasing*
WIP recovery	*Reconcile system stock with physical stock from copy picking lists*
Workarounds	*Encourage use of web ordering (automatic processes). Use manual picking lists (warehouse to notify shortages to purchasing)*
Backlogs	*Overtime*

Resource name		Resource type	Confirm
OOPS	*A*	*Application*	
BOS (Back orders)	*A*	*Application*	
Sales target system	*A*	*External supplier*	
Warehouse – picking	*I*	*Internal dependency*	
Purchasing	*I*	*Internal dependency*	
Post Office	*X*	*External dependency*	
Telephone system	*X*	*External dependency*	
...			

Note   All the text that is filled in, or verified by the user is in italic.

Table 5b   Activity data form

This form was developed as a database application and was presented to BC coordinators by the BC manager for discussion and immediate update.

This enabled immediate summary reporting of staff numbers by time period and by department or division. The activity lists were sorted by urgency and extracted into the corporate BC plan and the individual departmental plans. In the event of an incident, this summary information (staff and urgency) could be manipulated by the BC team to model the actual circumstances of staff availability and business priorities.

The application information took the RTO of the most urgent activity that used it, was sorted and given to IT to determine the prioritization of their application recovery. Internal dependencies created a high-level process map and the external dependencies were given to contract managers to review SLAs and contracts.

This form holds the basic Operational BIA data in a form suitable for this organization and could be adapted for other needs.

Additional operational data

In addition to the basic data, future reviews could attempt to collect more information that would be useful in devising or verifying strategies. Such information could include:

- home locations and journey to work (to enable the effect of localized or transport disruptions to be assessed);
- available skills (from other posts or companies) that might be used for redeployment during staff shortages;
- home working capability.

It is recommended that this information is collected with one topic per BIA update to avoid overwhelming respondents.

This example, added to the standard BIA form above, investigates the feasibility of running some activities from home.

Additional information on home working

Q1. Please enter 0–4 HERE=> _

    0=Activity must take place on site
    1=Activity could be partially run remotely
    2=Activity could be fully run remotely if technology allowed
    3=Activity can already be run remotely if necessary
    4=Activity is already run remotely sometimes/always

Q2. What is the minimum level of technology to run ALL applications required to run this activity remotely (please contact IT for clarification if necessary)?

Please enter 0–4 HERE=> _

    0=Not known

1=Technology not available
2=No technology required
3=Blackberry
4=Token
5=VPN software + token

Q3. How many staff doing this activity currently access applications remotely using:

VPN software and Token	
Token only	
Blackberry	
No technology required	
Do not access remotely	

Q4. For those who do not currently access applications remotely ONLY. How many:

Are willing to work from home	
Have a PC at home	
Have Broadband	
Have a 3G mobile	

Note: If it is not possible to split Q3 & 4 by activity then summarize by department on one activity sheet

Q5. Please comment on the feasibility of home working for this activity (non-technical issues)

The conclusions from the data collected from the organization using the above survey was that:

- home working was not feasible because of the nature of some activities (obviously most security and maintenance functions, but also some where teamwork was an important element);
- a considerable investment in existing capacity of remote access equipment would be required to make a significant difference to home working capabilities;
- further investment would be required to enable some applications to be accessed remotely, and some would not work remotely for technical reasons;
- many staff were keen to work from home but few of the staff, who were undertaking the most urgent activities that could be done from home, owned the appropriate equipment (Broadband and PC); therefore the organization would need to pay to install such facilities in their homes. This was difficult to justify in the not-for-profit sector.

> This challenged the currently held view of senior management
> that home working was a viable strategy with minimal
> investment.

Other operational data

Further information may be collected at this time from the appropriate
sources to assist the validation of the resource data and development of
operational recovery plans from this data. This may include:

- IT applications list – with planned recovery time if available;
- IT back-up and restoration strategies;
- IT DR strategy;
- lists of suppliers from accounts and procurement plus contracts,
  where applicable;
- HR policy and practice relating to staff relocation and redeployment;
- the likely response of staff to relocation or exceptional working
  practices (such as home working);
- existing alternative locations – their capacities and facilities;
- maintenance or support contracts – timescales consistent with MTPDs.

> An organization had cancelled its contract for out-of-hours IT
> support but would then have been unable to meet its
> commitments to customers if the resolution of an overnight
> problem was not started until 9.00 the next morning.

Analysing the Operational BIA data

There are several cross-checks that can be made on the resource data:

- Do the number of staff assigned to each activity add up (roughly) to
  the departmental staff numbers?
- Do the numbers required over time (using the BIA results) match
  existing work area recovery plans?
- Do the IT applications identified for each activity relate closely to the
  applications list from IT (there is often a huge discrepancy!)?
- Are there any obvious discrepancies between the IT back-up strategy
  and the MTDL of the activity's data?
- Does the list of equipment said to be required bear any relation to
  the equipment currently in use?
- Does the consolidated list of suppliers match that available from
  accounts or procurement?

- Do the supplier contracts match the expectations and requirements of the activities?

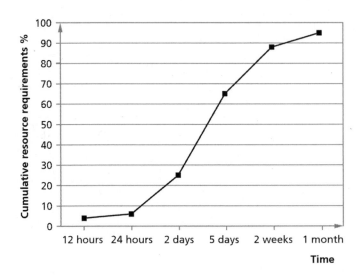

Figure 13   Staff resources required after an incident

Reporting the Operational BIA data

The Operational BIA is not usually reported separately to management; instead its findings result in a set of consolidated data that feed into the BCM strategy and recovery plans. Collecting information using a database form as shown in Table 5b enables consolidated data to be provided in a different level of accumulation (by department) and in different orders (by urgency).

Dept	Ref	Activity	Normal staffing	Day					
				0	1	3	5	10	30
PIN	1	Telephone enquiry / switchboard	3	5	5	3	3	3	3
PIN	2	Information (regular)	2	0	0	0	2	2	2
PIN	3	Resource materials	1	0	0	0	0	0	1
PIN		Total staff	6	5	5	3	5	5	6

Table 6   Departmental summary of staff requirements for Public Information (PIN) Department

In addition there may be two reports or sets of memos that come out of the Operational BIA which may be delivered to the appropriate management:

1. 'Obvious' threats report: this is where any observations on mitigating specific threats noticed during the BIA should be noted. It could identify issues such as urgent activities with a dependence on individuals or equipment, unsecured documentation or lack of security. It can add value to the BIA, but great care must be taken that its findings do not detract attention and budget from the wider BCM programme.
2. Process improvement report: where, during the BIA, examination of the activities has identified possible improvements in their operation which could increase efficiency or resilience.

7 Outcomes from the BIA programme

The principal output of the BIA is the quantitative information on timescales and resource requirements that will be used to determine appropriate recovery strategies for the organization.

However, there is other significant information that can influence not only the BCM programme but may also result in changes within the business.

Threat assessment

The step that follows the BIA in the BCM programme looks at the threats that could cause an incident by disrupting the organization's activities.

The BCM approach to threat assessment is to look at the urgency of the activity that will be disrupted if the threat occurs. Therefore this step must follow, not precede, the BIA.

The threats identified in this step are usually at an operational detail level, such as equipment failure or the spotting of single points of failure in the delivery of utilities. For example, the telephone service to an emergency helpdesk will attract more attention than that to a marketing department. Even if protection is put in place for the helpdesk telephone service there should be an insistence that a recovery strategy is still required in case the protection measures fail.

The more generic threats – such as fire, flooding or denial of access – do not need to be identified and assessed since it is assumed that the BCM strategies and plans will provide the appropriate response to these and the many others that could occur.

DC recovery strategies

The information collected in the BIA is the main determinant of recovery strategy and mitigation measures because it:

- determines the maximum timescale within which the strategy must be effective (MTPD);
- quantifies the scale of that strategy (number of resources) required at each stage of a recovery;
- identifies the most urgent activities where threat reduction is likely to be most beneficial.

> Almost all the services of a property portfolio management company – billing, purchases, sales and routine maintenance – were found to have an MTPD of several weeks because of the long-term investment nature of the managed assets. Only the tenant helpline was very urgent, but was regularly switched to a management company out of hours, so it could be handled by them during an incident.

Recovery time objective

Before the BIA results can be used a further step is required. The MTPD is, by definition, the point at which impacts are intolerable but the organization will probably not want to leave recovery to this point since it leaves no margin for comfort. Instead, for each product, service and activity a 'recovery time objective' should be set, as shown in Figure 14. This will obviously not be longer than the MTPD but may be shorter, depending on a number of factors such as:

- confidence in the estimate of the MTPD;
- dependencies of other activities – an activity pivotal to others should be recovered earlier;
- complexity of recovery – to allow for unanticipated problems to be resolved;
- smoothing out of recovery requirements and logistics over the recovery period.

The challenge is not to set the RTO too aggressively since, in general, the faster recovery solutions are the most expensive to implement and maintain, thus saddling the organization with an ongoing and unnecessary cost penalty.

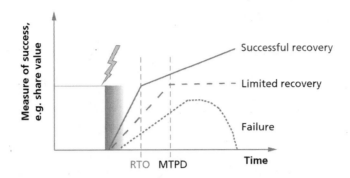

Figure 14   Setting the recovery time objective

Recovery strategies

An appropriate recovery strategy can be selected for each P&S such as:

- recover the process
- sub-contract all or part of the process.

Then, suitable tactics can be selected for each activity to satisfy its RTO and scaled by its resource requirement, as illustrated in Figure 15.

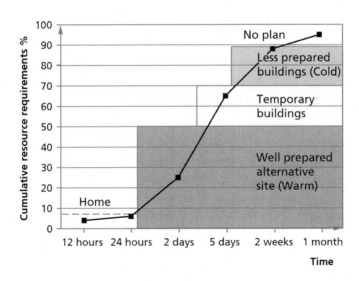

Figure 15   Matching RTO and resource requirements to strategy

Data back-up strategy

The requirements for backing-up information come from the MTDL (described earlier in Chapter 2) which identifies the required currency of the data – that is, how much data can tolerably be lost. In the same way that the RTO is set earlier than the MTPD, the recovery point objective (RPO) should be set conservatively later than the MTDL. For example, if the organization estimates it can just recover if it loses three days of data, then overnight (daily) back-ups should suffice.

This same technique should be applied to paper records and will help to decide whether some form of document management system should be implemented. The problems that would be caused by loss of work-in-progress documentation (such as cheques or customer documents), discovered in the BIA, should be followed up.

The loss of archived paper records is a different problem, where the impact of not being able to refer to the historical data contained in them may, or may not, have significant financial or reputational consequences. This complex issue tends to be addressed as a separate project in the BCM programme.

In practice, identifying the MTDL of every data set is a huge and unnecessary task. It is usually sufficient to verify that IT at least take daily back-ups off-site, and then only identify activities the data for which requires an RPO of less than one day – where alternative back-up strategies will be required.

Staff and skills

The BIA will identify urgent activities that are being undertaken by small teams with particular skills. Suitable strategies for these activities may include:

- cross-training of staff from less urgent activities;
- source a supplier who can take over the activity rapidly (and use them regularly);
- split the team across two or more locations.

The appropriate strategy may depend on training time and staff availability.

Evaluating supplier BC plans

The BIA may focus attention on suppliers of goods or services that could create problems if they experienced a disruption. The BIA enables the BCM programme to focus on those suppliers whose failure would most quickly cause difficulties – though single source supplies should also be investigated. Suppliers' BC plans should be inspected to ensure they can meet the timescales required.

> A manufacturing company was held to ransom by a supplier of leather who had given one month's notice as allowed in the contract (as a result of a change in fashions the supplier could earn more from selling the leather to the fashion industry). The process to verify the quality and colour of leather from a new supplier was known to take three months; the original supplier was therefore able to drive a hard bargain to continue supply for an additional two months.

Risk mitigation measures

It has been a long-standing challenge in BCM to demonstrate how the outcome of a BIA can be integrated with the results of any risk or threat assessment in formulating a BCM strategy.

The BIA provides an understanding of how an organization would be impacted by the failure of a process, but it cannot, on its own, provide a justification for risk mitigation measures, such as sprinkler systems and generators, that aim to prevent particular types of incident. To justify the purchase of these measures through cost–benefit analysis requires unverifiable assumptions about the frequency and extent of these specific events. However, the expenditure may be justified if there is a consequent reduction in insurance premiums or if the measure provides other benefits to the organization.

However, the protection of the urgent activities remains a responsibility for the BC manager and the BIA can identify how best to spend the budget that remains once other BCM strategies are in place.

Writing the plan

The BIA is not a plan in itself; nor does it contribute much material to the incident management plan or emergency response plan. As shown above, the main purpose of the BIA is to provide a requirements definition for the selection of BCM strategies and tactics that will be used to recover processes and activities, by the individual departments under the direction of a Recovery Team or Business Continuity Team.

The key direct contribution of the BIA to BCM plans is in providing the default activity recovery timetable for whichever plan (often called a

BCM Recovery or Continuity Plan) will enable the Business Continuity Team to coordinate the recovery of activities and manage recovery resources. Once RTOs have been set for each activity, with due regard to their MTPDs, then this prioritized list should form an early section in the recovery plan. In some organizations this can be used by the team with minor adjustments (mostly of periodic activities); in others (those where projects or events form a significant part of delivery) it is a starting point for establishing the required recovery timetable – and some notes regarding dynamic prioritization may be useful to the team. However, only a summary should be included in the plan, not the whole BIA.

Invocation decision

As well as determining recovery strategy, the information collected in the BIA can also assist with one of the key challenges of recovery: when to make a decision to invoke. This further supports Bill Meredith's 'backbone' statement quoted in the Preface.

If a whole site is destroyed, then it is obvious that recovery plans are put into place immediately. However, many disruptions are not destructive and, once resolved, can allow operations to resume rapidly – the power cut may end, the police may allow access, the strike may be called off. The continuity challenge is that the duration of the incident is usually unknown or the prediction of its resolution unreliable.

In the BIA we estimated an MTPD and then used it to set an RTO for each activity. We should also know how long the chosen recovery strategy for the activity takes to return it to full operation. When an incident of unknown duration occurs, we can determine from the RTO when the activity needs to be operational, and then work out how long that will take to achieve. This gives us the decision point – the latest point at which an invocation will enable recovery within the RTO. A decision before this point is not necessary – the situation may be resolved. Once this point is passed the option to use the recovery strategy has passed and there is only hope left that the situation will be resolved before the RTO! Knowing the decision point can prevent management making a premature decision in their panic.

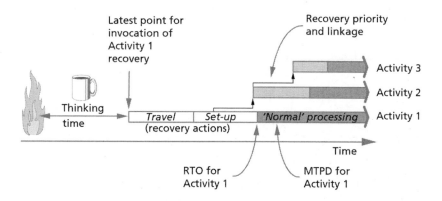

**Figure 16   How fixing the MTPD in the BIA and then the RTO helps the
timing of the invocation decision**

> On a routine Saturday morning check a security guard found
> water pouring down office walls from a burst tank in the roof.
> The senior managers were called and decided to invoke their
> recovery contract. The IT manager then reminded them that it
> was 48 hours before the offices were required for business and
> the contracted recovery work area would take less than 12
> hours to make ready, though it should be put on standby. Mops
> and buckets were acquired and by Sunday afternoon sufficient
> space was usable for them to stand down the recovery supplier.
> Had the IT manager not intervened, the organization would
> have incurred significant and unnecessary cost and disruption
> by relocating and having to move back again.

BCM awareness

There is also a considerable amount of 'soft' knowledge which will be
assimilated by those undertaking the BIA and may not be documented.
However, it is invaluable in planning the next steps in the BCM
programme. This knowledge includes:

- the current capabilities of incident response – including incident and
  media management, contracted services, emergency procedures –
  which will highlight training requirements;
- the existing level of awareness of staff and management, which will
  determine the extent and targets of a BCM awareness programme;
- identification of individual members of staff who could be interested
  in, or even enthusiastic about taking on roles within the response
  teams or as departmental BCM coordinators.

A Practical Approach to Business Impact Analysis   111

If an external consultant is employed to undertake a BIA, the importance of this information should illustrate why it is vital to allocate a member of staff to their team to capture this soft knowledge.

Improving the business

The BIA can result in benefits to the business beyond ensuring that its recovery strategies are appropriate. These include identifying:

- inefficiencies in processes – in particular where information is passed between departments;
- BCM recovery strategies that also provide benefits during normal business;
- unnecessarily tight timescales for processes that could be eased by redesign or reschedule;
- improvements in processes or resilience that can be incorporated during planned changes.

> An agency for temporary staff was looking to ensure that its enhanced IT DR was appropriate for the business. It was aware that it retained the best agency staff on its books by ensuring they were well supported and promptly paid.
> It ran a complex timesheet data entry and processing procedure for the first three days of each week with a deadline of Wednesday noon to allow time to send the data to a bureau for the payroll to be run that evening. On a couple of occasions this deadline had been missed, with serious repercussions and the company was concerned that temporary staff would go to other agencies if their pay was not processed. Because of the highly variable hours worked by each individual it would have made the situation worse to repeat the previous week's payroll. A new web-based system would allow the agency staff to enter their own timesheet data and the same deadline of Wednesday noon was proposed. Following the BIA it was suggested that giving the agency staff a Tuesday noon deadline would allow the payroll to be transmitted a day earlier, thus providing a spare day in which to resolve any problems.

Personal development

It is always fascinating to find out how an organization works at the tactical level; it is a view that no one else in the organization has. The CEO has a strategic view but, except in a small organization, a limited knowledge of how things are done. Below that, everyone is in a hierarchy which creates departments with little formal interrelationship except at an operational level.

This knowledge of the organization is powerful. It can be used to identify improvements and efficiencies that are not apparent from a departmental perspective. You may aspire to a position in the organization higher than that of a BCM, rewarding though it is. Using your unique knowledge of the business gained through the BIA is a legitimate way of career advancement.

8 Reflection

Looking back through the text, I realize that I have never followed the guidance I have given in its entirety. This is partly because the method has evolved over the years and also because every organization is different and each requires a unique approach. As a result, the guidance offered should be seen as an initial structure that will need to be adapted as knowledge of the organization grows, and not a straightjacket into which to force fit an analysis.

For those who are disappointed that no universal BIA template has been provided, the Appendix that follows provides a summary from which a customized template can be built.

Appendix 1

Consolidated Tactical and Operational BIA form

The text should have made clear why a standard BIA template cannot be given. In addition, for clarity, the tactical (urgency) and operational (resource) parts of the process have been separated in the text.

However, for those conducting a BIA for the first time, or where a consolidated Tactical and Operational BIA is appropriate, the following framework for developing a BIA interview form is offered. Refer to the relevant chapters in the text above for further explanation.

Completed by/date:	
Department	
Name and description of activity	A brief description of the purpose of the activity. Classification: Continuous / Periodic / Project / Other
Process	Process of which this activity is part (or the whole). Urgency of process should be copied from Tactical BIA
Products and services supported	Products and services supported (if specific) with their urgency copied from the Strategic BIA
Impacts of disruption	Use table of impacts/time from Strategic BIA for relevant P&S for verification and context • Enable additional impacts to be added, if relevant (and to be reconsidered at strategic level if significant) • Note variations/periodicity of impacts due to season, payment or regulatory timescales • Identify quantitative details of impacts (e.g. contract penalties) • Validate conclusions of Strategic BIA, or explore differences of opinion

Timescales of recovery	Time factors in recovery of the activity (depends on type of activity): • Process start-up time (warm up, data recreation, etc.) • Process time – from input to output • How long might backlogs take to clear • Therefore maximum tolerable period of disruption (taking above factors into account)
Interdependencies and supplies	Table of inputs and outputs • Classified by internal and external dependencies • Identify suppliers • Identify time issues – spare time, buffer stocks, contractual issues • Explore alternatives and time issues of using them
Resource requirements	Table of normal resource requirements (which may include): • Staff, IT equipment, equipment, data, IT applications etc. • Minimum data currency (this should exclude common resources e.g. power, standard desktop) If activity can be operated at a reduced level(s):* • Table of reduced level resource requirements • Time operation at reduced level is feasible (+ reason) • Working instructions on how to operate/manage reduced level * see earlier text as to why this is not recommended
Alternatives and workarounds	Alternative ways of working (may include) and drawbacks: • Manual processes (no IT) • Contractors • Working from home
Work in progress	Potential loss of data not yet backed up and of working documents – and procedures to recover, if necessary
Backlogs	If backlogs of processing will build-up, how these might be managed on resumption: • Overtime • Additional staff • Prioritization

Obvious threats (optional)	Perceived vulnerabilities in current processes (these may include): • Issues exposed by recent incidents • Tight deadlines or excessive pressures • Insecure work environment (open shelves, poor security) • Staffing issues (absence, concerns)

Appendix 2

Bibliography

British Standards

BS 25999-1:2006, *Business continuity management — Code of practice*

BS 25999-2:2007, *Business continuity management — Specification*

International Standards

ISO 31000:2009, *Risk management — Principles and guidelines*

ISO/DIS 22301, *Societal security — Preparedness and continuity management systems — Requirements*

ISO/CD 22313, *Societal security — Business continuity management systems — Guidance*

American National Standards

BCM.01:2010, *Business continuity management systems — Requirements with guidance for use*

Australia/New Zealand Standards

AS/NZS 5050:2010, *Business continuity — Managing disruption — Related risk*

Other publications

Nassim Taleb, *The Black Swan* (London, Penguin, 2007)

Good Practice Guidelines (London, Business Continuity Institute, 2010)

Terry Pratchett, *The Light Fantastic* (London, Corgi, 1986)